La

An Examination of the Gifts of the Holy Spirit

Rachel K. Sledge

Table of Contents

Dedication

To my loving parents: thank you for cultivating and encouraging me in Faith. Thank you for the opportunities to step out into the ministries you believed God was calling me. Thank you for shepherding my heart to love God and to pursue His Will above all else. Thank you for late nights working through difficult theological concepts.

To my gracious pastor: thank you for the grace you have given an entire congregation and generation to explore and experience the presence and baptism of God's Holy Spirit. Thank you for always seeking God in how to teach and lead your flock. Thank you for being sensitive to the Holy Spirit and the supernatural manifestation and ministries in our church.

To my wild African friends: thank you for listening to the sound of God's voice as He led you to America and a tiny United Methodist Church surrounded by farmland. Thank you for blowing on that small fire in my childheart so long ago and being a consistent encouragement to the life God has called me. Thank you for yielding yourselves up to God to minister His Holy Spirit to churches with no fire burning.

To my Firestarters: May you always remember that Faith comes by hearing and hearing comes by the Word of God. May you find the childlike confidence that a good Father gives good gifts. May you not be distracted by what people think of your unwavering faith. May you be willing to humbly explore all the Holy Spirit wants to do in and through you. Go start a fire!

Preface

In college I studied philosophy and in many ways it has influenced the way that I examine and think about God. I'm not interested in theologies that are legalistic and often a poor application of Scripture based on a biased or prejudiced understanding of God's character. True to my academic training, I try to start at the beginning and see where I end up. I try to ask questions of my own thoughts and then answer them with Scripture. I am not a theologian, but the following chapters are my theological conclusions from philosophical examinations. I wasn't always a student of philosophy. I was once a child who experienced God's supernatural power and that is where I begin.

These are my own examinations. Some of my conclusions may be different from your own. All I ask is that you consider what truth God may want to reveal to you through this book. Be wary the blinding lie of omission that Satan sows. The devil distracts us from the Truth and causes us to question God. That fallen angel began with questioning God's authority and that serpent sowed a seed of doubt in Eve. That devil questioned what God really said and what He really meant when He gave Adam and Eve instructions for holy living. Satan is still at work redirecting our understanding of what God really said and he works to deceive us into compromise.

There is power untapped by the Church because we have allowed Satan to constantly persuade us to compromise between the natural world and the supernatural world. Jesus called us to a life of living on the natural earth, but in the supernatural world. I hope that the following examinations release truth into your spirit and you begin to access power from above for your life.

My prayer for this book is to reveal truths hidden. My prayer is that faith rise up in you to see God in His glory and power magnified to this world through the Church. Christ's death on that cross and resurrection three days later affords us righteousness and access to the throne room of God the Father to make our requests known. Christ left for heaven so that the Helper, Holy Spirit, could come and work through the Church to bring the Gospel of Jesus Christ to a dying world. We must know what weapons and tools are available to us. We must begin to work and move in the Spiritual Gifts poured out at Pentecost.

May this book light a path of understanding to the manifest presence and power of God through His Holy Spirit. May you be encouraged and spurred on in your faith. If you have not already received the Baptism of the Holy Spirit, I pray that He be ever present with you as you read this book and may you reach out to receive all that Jesus purchased for you on the cross at Calvary. May you experience an increased thirst for more of the Holy Spirit and begin to move in the Spiritual Gifts to see God glorified and to show the world His true nature and character.

Lamplighting
The Baptism of the Holy Spirit

"No one, after lighting a lamp, puts it away in a cellar nor under a basket, but on the lampstand, so that those who enter may see the light." Luke 11:11 NASB

I love this verb, "lamplighting." Taken literally, well of course, lamplighting was at one time a profession of lighting street lamps. Often these "lamplighters" served as town watchmen mostly due to their presence among town streets at night. They were in some sense not too different from the watchmen of Isaiah 62:6. A lamplighter provided light and safety to those walking the town's streets at night.

Lamplighting can simply be lighting the path, bringing light to the way in which one should travel. Lamplighting should be the activity of the Church to a world lost in darkness. *"Let your light shine before men in such a way that they may see your good works, and glorify your Father who is in heaven (Matthew 5:16 NASB)."* Christians should be lighting lamps. They should be proclaiming the Word of God, illuminating the difference between the choking darkness of Satan's lies and the liberating light of God's Truth. Preachers should not be cowering to culture, but establishing a reputation for teaching the Gospel, preaching salvation and deliverance from this present darkness.

Likewise, within the four walls of a Church or the community of gathering believers there should be lamps burning with the fire and glory of God. The early Church was passionate about sharing the Gospel and one another's needs, both physical and spiritual. What about lighting lamps in the Church? Is Jesus still setting hearts aflame? Is the Church still burning to see Jesus be made known throughout the world and to return in

Glory? John the Baptist was said to be a burning and shining lamp to the Jewish people (*John 5:35*). No one can deny the incredible impact John had on the world. He boldly preached the truth of the Word of God. David expressed in Psalm 119 that the Word of God lights the path. John was a lamplighter. He took the truth that burned inside him and ignited others with a passion to see Jesus glorified as the Son of God. He called others to repentance, to be washed of their sins, turn away from the darkness and walk into the light of Christ.

John said that he would baptize with water, but there was someone coming who could baptize with the Holy Spirit and fire. John recognized it was Jesus when Christ came to the Jordan River to be baptized. Christ is the original lamplighter. On Pentecost tongues of fire appeared over the heads of those sitting in the upper room. He literally baptized them with the Holy Spirit and fire. Fire came down from heaven and hovered over their heads. Genesis Chapter 1 describes the Holy Spirit as hovering over Creation. In the Upper Room, the Holy Spirit burst through the doors, hovered over those 120 disciples, and filled them up with a Baptism distinct from the baptism John was doing at the Jordan.

Water baptism is an outward sign, a public confession and proclamation that Jesus is Lord over your life. This baptism comes after salvation; it does not make salvation. It is an individual's symbolic act meant to illustrate their act of faith to entrust their life in the nail pierced hands of Christ. Water baptism is a public opportunity for other Christians to rejoice with you in your salvation. Peter believed that water baptism was important for Christians and it often preceded the Baptism of the Holy Spirit in Scripture. In fact, Peter preached this on Pentecost to the Jews in Jerusalem right after the disciples were baptized by fire in the Upper Room.

The Jews were so convicted by the preaching they heard in their native languages that they asked Peter what to do. His instructions were: *"Repent and be baptized every one of you in the name of Jesus Christ for the forgiveness of your sins, and you will receive the gift of the Holy Spirit (Acts 2:38 ESV)."* However, water baptism is not a requirement for eligibility to be Baptized in the Holy Spirit. Remember, water baptism is simply an outward act on the part of a Christian, but Baptism in the Holy Spirit is an inward act of the Holy Spirit.

Baptism by fire is as thrilling as it sounds. The first sign given in Scripture is as the disciples were Baptized in the Holy Spirit they began to speak in other languages, which were not their native language. For what purpose did they begin to speak in unknown languages? The disciples were baptized with fire to light lamps in the hearts of the Jewish people by bringing the Word of God, a lamp and light by which to walk through this life. King David understood the value of the Word before it came in the form of Christ. He declared in the Psalms: *"Your word is a lamp to my feet and a light to my path (Psalm 119:105 ESV)."* There were many Jews visiting Jerusalem to celebrate Shavuot, a holiday to remember the giving of the Law to Moses, the giving of God's Word, on Mt. Sinai. On this day, Peter and the disciples were able to preach the Gospel of Jesus, the living Word of God, to the Jewish people in each of their native languages. It was essential for the disciples to receive the Baptism of the Holy Spirit, that baptism by fire, so they could preach the truth to visiting Jews.

Jesus did not just baptize those disciples by fire for that flame to flicker and fade. They went out to the nations of the known world igniting people groups, Jews and Gentiles, with the truth of salvation by faith in

Jesus Christ. Those lamps were used to light other lamps along the years. Jesus is still interested in a Church that is a burning and shining lamp illuminating the Truth. He is still baptizing in fire. Like the shamash of the hanukkiah, the menorah of Hanukkah, Jesus is the servant candle, the light of the world, setting His Church ablaze with the fire of His Holy Spirit. The Baptism of the Holy Spirit on Pentecost was not a temporary impartation of the manifest glory, presence, and power of God. It is still available for the workings of His supernatural power to testify of His love. Peter explained on Pentecost that the Baptism of the Holy Spirit is a promise for everyone who responds to the Gospel by the repentance of their sins and a public confession at water baptism (*Acts 2:39 NASB*). The Baptism of the Holy Spirit is not about the baptized, as it is with water; it is about the glory and power of God being made manifest in this world at this moment.

The disciples had committed themselves to a life of repentance, continued to share the teachings of Christ with those who wanted to hear, and they waited in anticipation of Christ's promise to send the Helper. How do you receive the Baptism of the Holy Spirit? Trim the wick, make sure the oil is fresh, and when a lamplighter comes by you'll be ready to receive the flame.

Before you can receive the Baptism of the Holy Spirit, you must receive salvation. To be sure, by salvation I mean the acknowledgement that you are a sinner and Jesus of Nazareth is the Messiah who died for your sins that you may live forever with Him in heaven. You must repent of those sins—make a willful choice to hate those sins and turn from them—and commit to observing God's commandments. Receiving salvation and receiving the Baptism of the Holy Spirit are two different events in the Christian life. We need both to walk in the fullness of Christ's victory. These two different events in a Christian's life are directly reflective of two very different historical Sundays.

On Easter Sunday, Jesus broke the old path to salvation available only to the Jewish people, a salvation by works, and established a new path to salvation. Paul explained that path simply: Confess Jesus is Lord and believe that God raised Him from the dead *(Romans 10:9)*. When this Truth is revealed to us, we transition from death to life. We receive new life, new breath, the in-breathed breath of God—the Holy Spirit. On Easter Sunday, Jesus opened the door for all people to receive salvation and eternal life in heaven. When you acknowledge the truth of Easter Sunday, you experience Easter Sunday first hand—you experience that same baptism into life. It has not grown old or stale; it is the same fresh breath of God breathed into your being—the core of your person—and it brings you to life.

On Pentecost Sunday, the disciples experienced another transition from the new life they received through Christ just fifty days earlier to a life of power through the Holy Spirit to overcome. Pentecost Sunday was a baptism into power. That truly describes the nature of Baptism in the Holy Spirit. Pentecost was the fulfillment of Acts 1:4-5, 8. This is where Christ's promise of the Baptism of the Holy Spirit and baptism into power is recorded for the disciples. From Acts 2 onward, the Book of Acts addresses receiving the Holy Spirit and it consistently refers to that experience on Pentecost Sunday. It was a metaphysical experience for the disciples. It went beyond their understanding of this physical world and their physical encounters with Jesus. They accessed the spiritual realm.

On Easter Sunday, the disciples experienced a resurrected Jesus. They saw Him, touched Him, spoke to Him. They were filled with the new life of God through Christ's sacrifice and the in-breathing of the Holy Spirit. On Pentecost Sunday, they experienced Jesus ascended and glorified. How? He promised that He was ascending to heaven and sending a helper. When that helper—the Holy Spirit—showed up in power, they experienced the greatness of the truth that Christ had ascended. They experienced an outpoured Holy Spirit. Before that moment, the Holy Spirit that they experienced through salvation was for the working of good in them. Now it was for the working of good through them. They were literally empowered to pour out onto others the revelation of Jesus. The result was and still is power.

This is perhaps why the Gospel's impact on the wider known world happens after Pentecost Sunday. The power of testimonies rippling out across the nations because of that Shavuot Sunday still causes the world to tremble at the power of the one true God. To be a lamplighter, you must have fire and to light the wicks of others comes through testimonies from real people's lives about topics we find difficult even as Christians. Christianity isn't just another religion with a doctrine.

Christianity is not mere theology or dogma. It is real because it follows a narrative of real people whose lives have been positively impacted by the life, death, and resurrection of Jesus. When we tell our stories of how Jesus changed us or reached us where we were, we need to be bare, unafraid, and unashamed to share the evidence. Otherwise, we're just story telling. Plenty of other religions are good at telling stories. We should share just the facts of our experiences and let the hearer decide whether he or she is open to receive the truth of what Christ has made available to him or her.

The Baptism in the Holy Spirit is not a sprinkling, a little flick of the Spirit; it is a total engrossment, enthrallment, and absorption in the Holy Spirit. The Baptism in the Holy Spirit completely immerses you and fills you up with the power of God and you can't but be used by Him to affect this world. The Baptism in the Holy Spirit means you're all in. Of course, with many things in life, going all in means giving some things up. No forgiven sin of the past disqualifies you from receiving the Baptism in the Holy Spirit. There are, however, hindrances, blockages, or prejudices that we have in our minds or unrepentance in our hearts that prevents us from receiving. To be clear, the Gospel teaches us that nothing we can do separates us from the love of God and God's love is shown through His giving of gifts—the Holy Spirit Himself and the Gifts of the Holy Spirit. Nothing we can do or have done prevents God from giving, merely us from receiving. To follow our lamplighting analogy, these spiritual hindrances are like having a wet wick—the lamp simply won't light.

So, what things can prevent us from receiving the Baptism of the Holy Spirit? First, thinking that it must somehow be earned. No gift is ever earned or deserved. God gives gifts because He loves and this is an outflow of His love for us. Moreover, because they are not trophies of character, God will not take them from you (*Romans 11:29*). If you think that you're not good enough to be God's mouthpiece or hands, remember Balaam's donkey (*Numbers 22:21-33*), the tax collector Matthew (*Matthew 9:9*), the adulterous murderer King David (*2 Samuel 11*), and a whole group of other people in the Bible that definitely weren't "good enough." God just wants us to be willing. Second, over thinking it. This is not an intellectual endeavor. In fact, the Baptism of the Holy Spirit makes you entirely reliant on Him because our human minds cannot possibly conceive or conjure up what the Holy Spirit wants to say or do in any given situation. You have to let go of your mind wanting to be in control. Third, unrepentance and unforgiveness can prevent us from receiving, as well. We know that sin separates us from God now just as it did in the Garden (*Isaiah 59:2*). Sin also creates a barrier for us to receive the gift God is giving to us. Unrepentance and unforgiveness in our lives indicate that we value holding on to those sinful thoughts or actions more than we value the freedom Christ is offering and the gift He wants to give.

How do you open up to receive the Baptism of the Holy Spirit? First, get rid of these hindrances. The Baptism of the Holy Spirit is only for believers and followers of Christ. So, repent and be baptized. This is Peter's instruction to the hearers of his Pentecostal sermon. In fact, Peter stated that if you do this, you're primed to "*receive the gift of the Holy Spirit (Acts 2:37-38 NASB)*." Next, you must ask for the Baptism of the Holy Spirit. If you ask for the Holy Spirit, God the Father will not let you down. He will never give you a snake when you ask for a fish. He will give you what you ask, because it is His will to give you the Holy Spirit. Ask for the Holy Spirit because He's already been promised to you (*Luke 11:9-13*). Lastly, you must actively desire, seek, and receive the Holy Spirit. Jesus said that we must be thirsty, come to Him, and drink of His living waters and the result will be living waters that flow out of us (*John 7:37-39*). John 7:39 is clear that the rivers of living water refer to the Holy Spirit.

If you want to receive the Baptism of the Holy Spirit, then you must first be thirsty. Thirsty for what? More than what you have through salvation alone—rivers of living water. Think about when you're thirsty. You desire only that which can satisfy and nothing else.

It is like that with the Holy Spirit. Out of desperation you must recognize that you need the Holy Spirit—more than what you received in water baptism. Being thirsty for the Baptism of the Holy Spirit means pressing forward until you find it and possess it. When you're thirsty, you go to the source—you find that well or that stream of clean, fresh water. Jesus is that endless well. He is the only baptizer in the Holy Spirit.

Throughout Scripture, Jesus repeated said to come to Him. In John 7:37-38, He specifically said to come to Him in order to receive the Baptism of the Holy Spirit. Just like at the well you must take the cup and drink the water in order to quench your thirst, so it is with the Baptism of the Holy Spirit. You must choose to receive the Baptism by a decision of your will. Just as drinking a glass of water is a conscious decision that requires physical action, so does receiving the Baptism of the Holy Spirit. You cannot passively drink water and you cannot passively receive the Baptism. When you choose to drink of the Baptism of the Holy Spirit, then you're all in and you are choosing to yield yourself up to the service of Jesus Christ even to be used by Jesus through your physical body. All of the Gifts of the Holy Spirit that are discussed in later chapters require us to yield up parts of our physical beings to be used by God for His glory and to make manifest His Holy Spirit.

How do you know if you received the Baptism of the Holy Spirit? You will know. It is unlike any other sensation this earth has to offer. You will know because that is exactly what you asked for, God promised this thing and He will fulfill His promises. Luke 11:13 makes it very clear that if you ask for the Holy Spirit, He will give it to you. If you ask for the Baptism in the Holy Spirit, you're not going to end up with something less than or nothing at all. Jesus described the nature of fathers to give their sons what they ask (*Matthew 7:9-*

11 and *Luke 11:11-12*), so too the Father of Creation will give to His sons. We are sons—children of God—who call to Him asking for good gifts and He responds by giving (*Romans 8:14-17*). If you ask for the things promised, you will receive them (*Matthew 7:7-8*).

There is one specific and distinct sign of the Baptism of the Holy Spirit: a vocal response. Many times I have heard people break out in uncontrollable joyous laughter, singing to Jesus, repeated praises to God, and even loud weeping. In Matthew 12:34, Jesus explained what is in our hearts will be made vocal by our tongues. When we receive the Baptism of the Holy Spirit we yield up control over our own bodies for His glory. Since so many verses in Scripture warn of the power of the tongue, it's no surprise that this is a member of our body that needs great direction from the Holy Spirit. It's also no surprise that this is the first aspect of our bodies that the Holy Spirit begins to control and use. Scripture identifies one particular vocal response consistently: speaking in Tongues.

The Book of Acts opens with a promise from Jesus that soon after His ascension the apostles would be baptized with the Holy Spirit (*Acts 1:4-5*). Fast forward a chapter and we are met with the infamous day of Pentecost. The record wastes no time in linking the Baptism of the Holy Spirit with beginning to speak in Tongues (*Acts 2:4*). This seals it for the apostles. There was no questioning whether they received the Baptism Jesus had told them about, because they began to speak in languages not known to their own minds.

This is a distinct experience in receiving the Baptism of the Holy Spirit because of their waiting. This is the only example given where people had to wait to receive the Baptism. Now, if you believe Paul as he wrote to Timothy in 2 Timothy 3:16, then you will understand that if there was an example of people having to wait or tarry or work for the Baptism of the Holy Spirit after Pentecost, then it would be a necessity to include such an example for the teaching, correction, and training of believers. Instead, we are given even more examples of speaking in Tongues as being the result or evidence of being Baptized in the Holy Spirit.

Paul clearly recognized speaking in Tongues as undeniable evidence of being Baptized in the Holy Spirit (*Acts 10:44-48*). These people weren't even "proper Christians" yet. They hadn't been baptized in water. Paul didn't wait to see if they had perfect understanding of the Gospel or if they were clothing the naked and feeding the poor; they were speaking in Tongues and it was Paul's understanding that this could only mean they were Baptized in the Holy Spirit and had obviously received salvation through faith in Christ. Then again in Acts 19:6, just like on the day of Pentecost, Tongues followed as an immediate sign of the Baptism in the Holy Spirit. No other distinctive sign of the Baptism of the Holy Spirit is given in the accounts of people receiving the Baptism. It is my conclusion that you will know if you have received the Baptism of the Holy Spirit when you begin speaking in Tongues.

Now, if you believe that you are thirsty, go to Jesus and drink. You may recite the prayer below, follow it as a guide, or pray in your own words and understanding asking for the Baptism in the Holy Spirit. Once you have prayed, breathe in the name of God (*Yahweh*): "Yah" (In) "Weh" (Out). Then, through faith, release your tongue to the control of the Holy Spirit. Begin to speak out. By an act of your will, open your mouth and move your lips. The Holy Spirit will do the rest and you will begin to speak in Tongues—a language unknown to your own mind.

Prayer to Receive the Holy Spirit

Lord Jesus Christ,

I acknowledge that You are the one, true Son of God. I thank You that You came and died on a cross for my sins, were buried, and rose from the dead. I ask You for forgiveness for the sins I have committed against Your Word, the Holy Scriptures. I believe that You have wiped my sins away and cleansed me of my wicked nature. I believe You when You say that I am an heir of Your kingdom.

I repent of any unforgiveness I have harbored in my heart. I release forgiveness now toward anyone with whom I have held resentment. If I have ever knowingly or unknowingly been involved in occult practices, I confess it is a sin, repent of my involvement, and renounce any influence or hold it may have on my life. I ask You to forgive me and plead Your blood over every aspect of my life that has been influenced by this involvement. I command all connections, physical and spiritual, that have been made from this involvement to be broken in the name of Jesus.

Jesus, I believe that only You can baptize in the Holy Spirit and with fire. I ask that You fill me up to overflowing, burn out the dross in my life, and use me to make manifest Your Holy Spirit and bring glory to God on Earth. I present myself to be used by You. Send me, Lord. I submit to You the members of my body and especially my tongue that it may sing a new song and worship You in Tongues of angels. Through an exercise of my will and by faith I receive this gift of the Baptism of the Holy Spirit now. Thank you, Jesus. You are worthy of all the glory and praise. Amen.

Words of
Wisdom and Knowledge
Psychic Power or Present Purpose?

*"For to one is given the word of wisdom through the
Spirit, and to another the word of knowledge according
to the same Spirit"*
1 Corinthians 12:8 NASB

A Word of Wisdom can be an encouragement in
what direction to take in life, perhaps even giving
wisdom as to when. This Gift operating in the Church
body is beneficial to the whole church. We should
desire this Gift as a help to our brothers and sisters in
Christ. This in no way is meant to dilute the power that
a Word of Wisdom may have on someone who is not a
committed Christian. For in fact, Words of Wisdom and
Knowledge may reach into the innermost thoughts,
concerns, and fears of someone without an intimate
knowledge or relationship to Christ and affect them in
a way that mere human words of wisdom never could
hope to achieve.

These words make the Wisdom and Knowledge of
God known through the manifestation of the Holy Spirit
as seen in the operation of the Gifts. Since our triune
God is invisible and imperceivable to the five senses,
when the Holy Spirit is manifested through the Gifts,
God makes Himself known in a physical world. To be
sure, just like the other seven Gifts whose explanations
are to follow, these Words of Wisdom and Knowledge
are supernatural. Our limited human perception of our
world, our understanding, and our education could
never muster the ability for us to produce such words
simply on our own.

These Gifts will be discussed together to help give understanding to their similarities and unique qualities to one another. Natural wisdom and knowledge often work in unison with each other. To have knowledge of our natural world often leads to wisdom in how to work and act in this world. Thought of more precisely, knowledge is information we obtain, or facts, and wisdom is the direction we take with that information or it gives us insight as to what to do with those facts. The Book of Ecclesiastes lends us a perfect example of this for further clarity: *"If the axe is dull and he does not sharpen its edge, then he must exert more strength. Wisdom has the advantage of giving success (Ecclesiastes 10:10 NASB)."* Wisdom helps us to accomplish life's tasks with clarity and a favorable outcome.

When we are speaking of supernatural Words of Wisdom or Words of Knowledge, which come only through the Baptism of the Holy Spirit, then we must understand that we cannot manufacture these Words from a storehouse of our own experiences. They are directly from God because they are uniquely His own Wisdom and Knowledge imparted to us momentarily for a specific situation, often only on a "need-to-know" basis. I use the words "momentarily," "specific," and "need-to-know" simply to emphasize that this Gift is only the impartation of a small portion of God's omniscience.

These Words are a crumb, if you will, of God's all-knowing, all-wise, and all-seeing mind. The Psalmist described the vastness of God's knowledge and wisdom with humanly uncountable things. For us to receive more than a word at a time, that is situation specific, may overwhelm us entirely. I think we may buckle under the weight of such an experience. God in His benevolence does not burden us with all of His wisdom or knowledge, but only what is beneficial or necessary in a specific situation.

A Word of Wisdom can be critical during ministry to another person. It will give the correct instructions for achieving the most beneficial result. Going back to that passage from Ecclesiastes, a Word of Wisdom can tell you to sharpen the axe and then where on a tree's trunk to start chopping. A Word of Wisdom gives foresight into the most advantageous and effective action to take. A Word of Wisdom helps us to have breakthrough in a situation that needed clarity and revelation of direction.

A Word of Wisdom can also be Scriptural Wisdom applied to a situation for which our natural person has knowledge. It takes an impartation of God's own Wisdom, however, to know which piece of Scriptural Wisdom is needed for the situation. We cannot operate in these Gifts without having received the Baptism of the Holy Spirit. You may be able to share godly, biblical wisdom with someone, but a Word of Wisdom will give supernatural direction straight from heaven. The proper use of wisdom is to make proper use of knowledge. Therefore, the manifestation of a Word of Wisdom will make proper use of our knowledge of Scripture for a specific situation.

A Word of Wisdom will help to create unity within a community of believers. This Gift can function on a particularly striking level of intimacy between to whom the Word is given (the receiver) and God. It will speak directly into a situation or circumstance, assuaging fears and confusion of the receiver, giving them victory to press forward in the right direction. A Word of Wisdom can then impart faith, confidence, and strength to the receiver to continue in a difficult direction.

A Word of Knowledge can serve as a diagnosis of a situation by identifying the cause or origin of the problem. For example, a Word of Knowledge could be the revelation of a certain sickness in a certain person. In this case I believe that a Word of Knowledge could be the catalyst of faith for that person to receive healing. In other words, that Word of Knowledge about a sickness could create faith or cause boldness to rise up in the receiver to receive healing. A Word of Knowledge could identify an event that brought about health issues. This could be an event that is directly related physically or it could be an event where something occurred emotionally or spiritually and created a gateway for sickness.

A Word of Knowledge can be the key to total freedom and deliverance for someone by identifying the root of the problem. God reaches out and touches an area in someone's life (mental, emotional, or physical) that needs to be identified, opened, and cleaned before healing can take place. Sometimes a Word of Knowledge is used to reveal truth in situations where there are lies that would prevent anyone from naturally being able to identify the truth. Sometimes a Word of Knowledge will come as proof of God's existence to a non-believer. The Word will specifically identify facts and details that the giver of the Word could not have possibly known about the receiver. A Word of Knowledge is a reminder that we cannot hide from God and it can come to bring healing to a person, deliverance, or even cause them to repent. It brings what is sometimes hidden into the light. A Word of Knowledge will ultimately be given to thwart the plans of Satan to destroy hope in God and the lives of believers.

I think it is helpful to note that there are Biblical examples of Words of Knowledge and Words of Wisdom given supernaturally to God's people before the Ascension of Jesus and the coming of the Holy Spirit on Pentecost. These records are limited because the Gifts of the Holy Spirit only come with the Baptism of the Holy Spirit. Therefore, any supernatural Knowledge or Wisdom that either comes in Scripture or the life of a believer prior to the Baptism of the Holy Spirit is not the Gift in operation. However, I do think that these examples are helpful in illustrating what the Gift will look like once you have received it.

It would seem that after the outpouring of the Holy Spirit the genuine accounts of Words of Knowledge and Words of Wisdom after Pentecost Sunday are too numerous to count. They can come in ministry in the most remote places, affecting lives with no worldly acknowledgement or glory. To give further clarity to the operation and nature of these Gifts, I will highlight several accounts in Scripture where these Gifts were in operation.

In Acts Chapter 15 an account is given regarding the Church's requirements on the Gentile believers to become bonafide followers of Jesus' teachings. This is the Church's first encounter with legalism. Believers from the Pharisees wanted to require Gentile converts to observe all the Jewish commandments—the law of Moses. The apostles and elders in Jerusalem held council to discuss this issue. James quoted from the prophet Amos and drew a conclusion, which by my estimation, could not have properly come about by James' own education, understanding, or wisdom. In fact, in many ways it is in direct contrast to what his training and experience would have taught him was wise. James received wisdom not to burden the converting Gentiles with Jewish law and requirements.

Paul earlier in the chapter reminded the Council that generations of Jews had failed to uphold the law of Moses in its entirety and that salvation comes through the grace of Jesus Christ only. This helped the Council to decide that it was overly burdensome to require of Gentiles what even Jews were unable to obey. Why do I categorize this as a Word of Wisdom? First, it takes the facts regarding humanity's ability to uphold the law of Moses and it provides direction as to what to do with that fact. Second, it is not what I would expect from a council of Jewish believers in Christ whose whole lives had been taught to observe the law of Moses and whose experiences in Judaism shaped their understanding of Christianity.

Another example of a Word of Wisdom, comes from Genesis 41:33-40. In this account, Joseph interpreted a dream for Pharaoh. We understand that God gave this dream to Pharaoh and its interpretation through Joseph as prophetic of what was to come. Proof of this dream being prophetic can be found in Genesis 41:47-57 as we read of the years of plenty and the years of famine. The wisdom that Joseph shared with Pharaoh takes the interpretation of the dream as a fact of what is to come and it gives Pharaoh a course of action to take. Joseph exercised immense wisdom in that situation, but having never faced those circumstances before, it is most likely that this wisdom came from God and not from Joseph's own education and experiences. In fact, this wise instruction helped to fulfill the prophetic promise of Joseph's own life. Joseph became a trusted leader in Pharaoh's court and more of Joseph's story unfolded true to his dreams as recorded in Genesis 37.

Solomon is perhaps the most famous receiver of God's Wisdom in Scripture. However, we should make note that he is unique as he received wisdom from God regularly. This is not his natural wisdom acquired through his education or experience. So, each example of Solomon exercising wisdom is to be understood as God's Wisdom. Solomon received a Gift of Wisdom,

God's own wisdom to judge wisely (*1 Kings 3:9-14*). He is an example of what this Gift will look like with the Baptism of the Holy Spirit. Although, verse 12 implies that the wisdom Solomon received was special and states that it will not be given to anyone after him. This seems to indicate that Words of Wisdom are only snippets of what Solomon would have received during his life on earth.

In 1 Kings 3:16-28 we are given the story of Solomon and the dispute between two mothers. Some might be horrified to think that Solomon's wisdom came in verses 23-25. I am skeptical that Solomon actually intended to cut the live boy in two. Rather, I choose to believe that Solomon had supernatural wisdom to know that this proposition would cause grief in the true mother. Indeed it did, because she cried out to let the baby live. The other woman, out of spite, said that neither should have the child. God's wisdom was in Solomon to judge and govern. However, this is an interesting twist on wisdom. Usually we mean it as guiding positively by giving explicit direction. Here, wisdom came by giving a negative option to highlight the true path to take. It showed that such a gruesome act would be unthinkable to the real mother.

Jesus' father, Joseph, received both supernatural Knowledge and Wisdom through a dream. Matthew 2:13a tells us what Joseph heard, *"Get up! Take the Child and His mother and flee to Egypt, and remain there until I tell you... (NASB)."* This was a Word of Wisdom given to Joseph; he obviously would have needed to explain this sudden exodus from Bethlehem to Mary. This was a Word of Wisdom because it gave specific direction and course of action to take regarding a specific fact. That fact came in the second part of verse 13, *"...for Herod is going to search for the Child to destroy Him (NASB)."* This part of the dream is a Word of

Knowledge. Joseph could not have known based on his own education or experience that Herod was specifically going to seek out Jesus to kill him. While Matthew 2:12 tells us that the magi were warned not to go back to Herod, nothing indicates that they were told why or that they shared their dream with Joseph. From this example we can understand that sometimes both Words of Knowledge and Words of Wisdom come tethered together or that one will follow the other to bring clarity or understanding. It is wisdom to flee to Egypt, if there is a reason to flee. That reason was revealed and supernaturally so, because in verse 16 we read that Herod commanded the death of male children under the age of two after he realized the magi were not coming back.

It is no surprise that Elisha received knowledge from God as His prophet. Elisha received supernatural Knowledge about the actions of his servant, Gehazi, to keep goods for himself through an act of deceit. In 2 Kings 5 Elisha gave instructions to Naaman in order to be healed of leprosy. Naaman wished to pay Elisha for the Healing, but Elisha would not accept it. After a short time, Gehazi conspired to go after Naaman and collect the payment on Elisha's behalf. When he returned to Elisha, the prophet *knew* in detail the transaction Gehazi had with Naaman. Elisha, without the power of the Almighty, could not have known where Gehazi had been, what he had been doing, and certainly not with the detail with which he knew it. Again, Elisha received a Word of Knowledge as Aram (Syria) waged war with Israel. In 2 Kings 6:8-12, the king of Aram told his servants the specific location of his encampment. Elisha received a Word of Knowledge regarding the exact location of the king of Aram and sent word to the king of Israel. When the king of Israel sent a word of warning to this place, the king of Aram became angry.

The king of Aram assumed there was a traitor among his servants. Again, Elisha could not have known where the king of Aram was going to camp. Elisha didn't have spies in Aram's army or among the king's servants. This knowledge came direct from heaven and helped aid Israel in avoiding the Aramean raiders this time.

Daniel, like Joseph, was given the interpretation of dreams of kings. In Daniel 2 Nebuchadnezzar, king of Babylon, had a troubling dream. He sought the interpretation of the dream from his sorcerers and other advisors. Nebuchadnezzar had one requirement: he would not tell them what he had dreamed, but instead they had to first tell him the dream and then interpret it. All his wise men and sorcerers were unable to tell him the dream. Nebuchadnezzar became angry and declared that all the wise men be killed. From chapter 1 we know that this included Daniel. When he discovered the call for all the wise men to be killed, Daniel went to the king's bodyguard to ask why. When Daniel discovered why, he requested time with the king and then sought a Word of Knowledge about the dream from God. Daniel supernaturally received Knowledge through a vision of Nebuchadnezzar's dream and then he gave the interpretation. Daniel's knowledge of the dream came as direct revelation from God.

The next two examples come from the life and ministry of Jesus. I use these examples because Jesus was fully reliant upon His relationship with the Father and the Holy Spirit in order to operate supernaturally while here on Earth. The book of John begins with Jesus' public ministry. In John 4:15-18 Jesus met the Samaritan woman at the well. It was during this interaction that Jesus received an explicit Word of Knowledge regarding this woman's marital status and history. She immediately recognized that it was the power of God speaking through Jesus, although she mistook Him for merely a prophet. Then Jesus identified Himself to her as the Messiah. This Word of Knowledge was so striking to this woman that she went down to the town and told more Samaritans of Jesus. Jesus was able to minister His gospel to Samaritans because of a simple Word of Knowledge. This group of Samaritans became followers of Jesus. "*It is no longer because of what you said that we believe, for we have heard for ourselves and know that this One is indeed the Savior of the world (John 4:42 NASB)*."

Later in the book of John, Jesus received a Word of Knowledge that Lazarus was dead (*John 11:11-17*). What's interesting about this example is that after Mary and Martha sent word to Jesus that Lazarus was sick He said in verse 4, "*This sickness is not to end in death, but for the glory of God, so that the Son of God may be glorified by it (NASB)*." Then just a few verses later Jesus said, "*Lazarus is dead, and I am glad for your sakes that I was not there, so that you may believe; but let us go to him (John 11:14-15 NASB)*." The Word of Knowledge in verse 14 is obvious. There is no natural way that Jesus could have known that Lazarus died. When Jesus received word from the sisters it just said that Lazarus was sick. Before Jesus even set out for Judea to visit Mary, Martha, and Lazarus it was revealed to Jesus that Lazarus was dead. Moreover, the purpose for Lazarus' death was supernaturally made known to Jesus.

One of the most stark examples of truth revealed where lies are told comes in Acts 5:1-11. This example comes after Pentecost Sunday and the receiving of the Holy Spirit. It highlights the importance a Word of Knowledge can have in keeping the Church honest by making them undeniably aware of God's omniscience. Those who became followers of Jesus in Jerusalem became part of a community, they were a body of believers whose hearts were attuned to the Holy Spirit and were in harmony with one another. Luke wrote that there was such generosity among the believers that no one was needy because those who had land and wealth would give their proceeds to be distributed among the congregation by the apostles (*Acts 4:32-35*).

Luke gave an example in verses 36-37 when Barnabas gave the proceeds from a field he had sold. In chapter 5 we learn that Ananias and Sapphira sold a piece of property, but they decided not to bring the total sum of the proceeds to the apostles. Ananias took that certain amount before the apostles, but Peter was not deceived. Peter received supernatural knowledge that the land sold for more than was put before him.

> *"Ananias, why has Satan filled your heart to lie to the Holy Spirit and to keep back some of the price of the land? ...Why is it that you have conceived this deed in your heart? You have not lied to men but to God." Acts 5:3-4 NASB*

Ananias died immediately. Three hours later, Sapphira came and told the same lie. She also fell down dead. Verses 11-13 explain that fear—reverence and awe— for God and His omniscience came over the Church and non-believers.

These examples from Scripture help to make clear the difference between Words of Wisdom and Words of Knowledge. Words of Wisdom are by nature a revelation of God's purpose, pointing the receiver in the direction of His will and plan for their life. Since these Words bring clarity in decision-making or action taking, they speak to the future. We already gain wisdom from the past (hopefully) as we grow, both as people in general and as Christians. As I've said above, this is God's own Wisdom imparted to someone and not wisdom that comes from their own experiences.

Just as natural wisdom and knowledge work together, so do these two Gifts.

A Word of Knowledge will be about something that has already happened in the past or is currently happening. It is a supernatural impartation of facts about a person or situation the giver could not possibly know on their own. As such it is important to understand that a Word of Knowledge is not future telling—strictly by definition, it is not prophecy itself— it is a revelation of facts either past or present. The examples of Knowledge make it particularly clear that this is not a prophetic gift, but a Spiritual Gift uniquely its own. They help to magnify the definition that it comes as a small piece of God's own Knowledge.

If a Word of Knowledge is imparted, a Word of Wisdom may also follow, so that the one operating in the Gift of Words of Knowledge knows what to do with that knowledge. For example, someone to whom Words of Knowledge are imparted by the Holy Spirit may receive wisdom that is not to be shared, but is imparted to incite intercessory prayer. As you begin to operate in these Gifts it always important to seek the Lord as to what should be done with these Words.

Faith
Belief, Character, or Confidence?

"to another faith by the same Spirit..."
1 Corinthians 12:9a NASB

Paul strategically listed Faith before the Gifts of Healings and the Effecting of Miracles. The Gift of Faith is supernatural; we cannot decide by our own will to have this kind of faith. We can, however, ask for the Holy Spirit to give us this Gift. Paul said that we should desire the Spiritual Gifts, and what good is desiring if we never receive?! The Gift of Faith is one that invites and then escorts the power of God into a situation. Those with the Gift of Faith are like ushers directing the faith of others to trust God and believe for the supernatural. The Gift of Faith is a catalyst for experiencing shaking of our earthly preconceptions. It is a fuel for hope and a bridge to the supernatural for us to experience and exercise the Gifts of Healing and the Effecting of Miracles.

An understanding of this Gift requires an understanding of what it is not. There can be three different applications of the word "faith" and the more clearly we understand two of them, the more clearly we understand the unique and powerful nature of "Faith" when describing the Gift of the Holy Spirit.

The word "faith" is commonly used when referring to a person's belief in God. This kind of faith is what every Christian must have to be a Christian. It's what Paul described to the churches in Galatia, *"yet we know that a person is not justified by works of the law but through faith in Jesus Christ... (Galatians 2:16a ESV)."* This kind of faith is the faith to basic salvation and a relationship with God. This kind of faith is most clearly defined in Hebrews 10:39-11:1 as the author wrote:

> *"³⁹But we are not of those who shrink back to destruction, but of those who have faith to the preserving of the soul. ¹Now faith is the assurance of things hoped for, the conviction of things not seen (NASB)."*

It is undeniable that we must have this kind of faith before we could ever hope to operate in the Gift of Faith. Without knowing from Whom the power comes, without that Abrahamic conviction that He is the one true God, we will not be able to exercise a Gift that demands reliance on that belief.

The second way we use the word "faith" is when we talk about the Fruit of the Spirit. Sometimes "faith" in Galatians 5:22 is translated as "faithfulness," because it is talking about the character that the Spirit develops in believers. The Fruit of Faith is what the Spirit produces in Christians as they grow in relationship to Christ and understanding of the Father's Will. Jesus chastised the scribes and the Pharisees because despite all their knowledge of the Law—their understanding of the covenant between God and the Hebrews—they failed to show any alteration in their character (*Matthew 23:23*).

The character of a friend is found in their faithfulness to us. Solomon wrote in Ecclesiastes that the faith of our friends is like medicine to us (*Ecclesiastes 6:16*). This use of the word "faith" speaks to the trustworthiness of our character; it is an evidence of the right relationship we have with God. Having the Fruit of Faith in our lives as Christians is what allows others to receive from us when we exhibit the Gift of Faith. If we have the Gift of Faith, but have not proven ourselves to bear any testimony of God's grace and mercy in our lives through the changing of our character, then we may become something to stumble over. Jesus said that the fruit we bear is evidence of our nature and the health of our fruit is evidence of our roots (*Matthew 7:1-17, 20*). So, may we prove faithful to our God by yielding a harvest of good fruit that testifies to the glory of God in our lives. As we grow in faith (belief), may we also grow in faith (faithfulness), so that we will walk in the power of Faith to see God move in supernatural ways.

The remaining kind of faith is the Gift of Faith. Faith requires that you lay down your selfish, fleshly preconceptions of God's Will in favor of a life abandoned to whatever He wills. This Faith isn't believing that you'll get exactly what you're asking for or what you want God to do. This Faith is an unwavering confidence that God is true to His character as we see time and time again. Different from the belief kind of faith that God has a character to be trusted, this faith is that God's way is not our way, but what He promised He will do. This is Abraham's faith when he trusted that God would provide the sacrifice. This Faith is what Abraham exhibited when he took his promised son up to a mountain to be sacrificed before God and chose to believe that either God would resurrect Isaac from the dead or supernaturally provide another animal to be sacrificed (*Genesis 22:1-18*). Abraham's faith was a conviction that God would perform His promises (*Romans 4:20-22*). Faith is a confidence of God's faithfulness and confidence is the present state of conviction and hope.

Those with the Gift of Faith have the expectation of God to move. When He does, they are not surprised. They trust in God's character first and they are not swayed by outcomes, because they understand that God is above all sovereign and good. They choose to believe His Word above all else and put faith in His faithfulness. The Gift of Faith is confidence in the power of God to affect the world around us and a vehicle to see that power manifest. As such it is God's own Faith imparted to us as believers by the Holy Spirit.

This Gift is to have the faith *of* God—divine and perfect—through a supernatural impartation to accomplish God's own purpose in a specific situation. To have the faith of God is not about a certain measure or amount of faith. It is about the value or concentration of faith—it is a matter of quality over quantity. This is the faith of a mustard seed—small and mighty, seemingly insignificant and yet, incredibly potent (*Matthew 17:20*). It's the faith of God Himself. When Mark recorded Jesus talking about the faith to cast a mountain into the sea, He said, *"Have faith of God... (Mark 11:22 YLT)."* The faith of God is a pure concentration that whatever is said in accordance with His Will will be done. James later said that a prayer of Faith has the power to heal the sick (*James 5:15*). It is God's own Faith to work the supernatural in the natural. The Gift of Faith is the faith to believe for God to do innumerable things in this world. If we can believe for Him to heal the sick, He has the Faith and has imparted that same faith to us for so much more to be done in this world.

God's Faith has determined, does determine, and will determine the destiny of this world. His Faith, given to us as a Gift, swells within us to respond when a measure of Faith is required to effect the circumstances that threaten to cut short the fate of individuals, groups, and nations. Faith's sole purpose is to be activated in circumstances where the people of God are called to ask for His intervention, so that through Faith, God's plan and Will may be accomplished in a certain situation. With God's Faith His Church has the ability to bring the power of Heaven here to Earth.

When God speaks, Creation snaps into existence. When Jesus speaks, Creation responds without delay. If we as the Body of Christ, seeking His Will, speak to circumstances and situations with the Faith of God, then what we say and what we do, under the power of the Holy Spirit, will be effective. We must understand, though, that it is only with the Holy Spirit, as one part of our triune God, that we could ever hope to affect this world as only He can.

We see this in the casting down of false gods as Elijah effectively called down fire from Heaven to consume an offering (*1 Kings 18:20-39*). Jesus' own ministry was filled with His confident words of Faith spoken with the authority of God to affect the circumstances of God's creation. Matthew and Mark both wrote accounts of Jesus cursing a fig tree (*Matthew 21:18-22* and *Mark 11:12-14, 19-25*). This example of Faith, expressed through words of authority, shows us the power that can come through words of Faith. These accounts provide us with an explanation as to how this was possible. Jesus extended that power and authority to any who have the confident Faith of God.

Since Faith is the Divine working through us to affect the world around us, we can understand that it is this Gift that is in operation in the casting out of evil spirits. Once an evil spirit is discerned and identified it takes a word of authority, spoken in Faith, to produce deliverance. We can imagine that it would take a concentration of the purest Faith to rend an evil spirit powerless to continue to hold onto its victim-host. To be considered in a different way, to separate a spirit from a body takes great authority and a confidence that when a word of deliverance is spoken it is done from the moment it leaves our lips.

Jesus' deliverance ministry clearly follows one specific pattern: a word of authority spoken in Faith. He left the spirits no option, but to leave their human host. Jesus' Faith was such that He confidently believed that He had the authority from His Father in Heaven to affect the presence of demons. We know from Matthew 10:1 that believers in Christ have been given that same authority through a commissioning from Christ to cast out evil spirits.

In Jesus' ministry and then in the ministries of Peter and Paul this is the Gift that is in operation to raise people from the dead. Dead people do not need Healing. They need a word of Faith, like that spoken during Creation, to cause life to enter back into their bodies and affect a Miracle. Jesus commanded dead people to "get up!" These were clearly words of authority spoken with Faith. There is no indication that Jesus questioned whether God could or would. Jesus understood that He had been given that authority and when the Spirit moved Him to act in Faith He did so confidently.

Sometimes the Gift of Faith comes through an act of absurdity. Paul learned from Elisha that the crazy act of laying on a dead body, believing for it to come back to life, was an effective absurd act of Faith. Elisha laid on top of a dead boy until the boy's body began to warm up again, finally the boy sneezed seven times and woke up (*2 Kings 4:1-37*). During Paul's ministry in Troas he was preaching late in the night and a man by the name of Eutychus drifted off to sleep and fell out of a third floor window to his death. Paul went down, fell on him, wrapped his arms around Eutychus, and declared, "*life is in him (Acts 20:7-12 NASB)*."

If we understand that 1 Corinthians 13 is the "Love Chapter," then when we begin to study Hebrews 11 we can see that it could be named the "Faith Chapter." Although we do not know for certain who wrote Hebrews, what is clear is that they understood the absurd Faith of Abraham. "*He considered God to be able even to raise someone from the dead, and as an illustration, he received him back (Hebrews 11:19 HCSB)."* Abraham acted in obedience to take Isaac to the mountain and his Faith is what led him to go in confidence that God would give Isaac back to him. This chapter in Hebrews relays how the Faith of those committed to belief in God acted in absurd contradiction to their circumstances and through that Faith had an incredible impact on history (*Hebrews 11:32-35*).

When a person of faith walks in the unshakeable belief that God *can* do anything it elevates a person with Faith to confidently expect that He *will*. Reading the accounts of Faith heroes in Hebrews 11 encourages us to believe for the absurd and this passage highlights so many great examples of people trusting in God's character, acting in the absurd with Faith, and seeing God work to shake circumstances. The people we find listed in Hebrews 11 faced impossible situations and yet their conviction in God's power and character fueled them with Faith to move mountains.

From the moment Moses discovered his true heritage and divine purpose, he was thrust into a choice of faith: would he walk in the confidence of God's character and act in Faith to accomplish what God wanted or would he stay in the wilderness? Perhaps even more, was Moses' brother Aaron whose absurd acts of Faith under his brother's directions brought about the ten plagues of Egypt. Both brothers held deep convictions that the God of Abraham, Isaac, and Jacob would keep His covenant with the Hebrew children. It was this belief in God's nature that propelled them to expect the supernatural.

Gideon's story of Faith slowly builds into total confidence in God's ability to affect this natural world through supernatural means. When the Angel of the

Lord first appeared to Gideon, Gideon expressed disbelief as to why the youngest son of the most insignificant family of the tribe of Manasseh would be chosen by God to defeat Midian. Gideon asked God for a sign that what He had promised would come true. The passage in Judges 6:36-40, I believe, is frequently misunderstood as Gideon lacking Faith. I suggest that this passage makes clear Gideon's Faith to believe God could move incredibly, but before he stepped out to do what he thought God was instructing Him to do, he wanted definitive confirmation. Gideon believed that if these instructions were from God, then only the fleece would have dew on it and not the ground. He believed that God had the power to do it. He believed that if he woke up to a dry ground and a dry fleece that he had not heard properly from God. Judges Chapter 7 gives the account of "Gideon's 300 Chosen Men" and it is clear that Gideon confidently trusted God to defeat Midian with only 300 men. Gideon had learned to be obedient to God and see impossible situations become possible.

David was so distraught by Goliath mocking God and the children of Israel that he was compelled to confront Goliath. David must have been acting from Faith. We don't know how big David was, only that he was the youngest brother, and perhaps not even a full-grown man. Yet, he chose to face a nine-foot tall behemoth of a man without a second thought. The glory of God was so important to David that he believed in God and acted in the absurd. He was essentially a child facing a warrior with a slingshot and five smooth stones. David spoke a word of authority in Faith to Goliath and he declared the result of their altercation. For David, he understood that the Lord would not suffer to be mocked and to allow the Hebrew children to be mocked. David declared, "...I will strike you down *and remove your head from you (1 Samuel 17:46b NASB).*" David had Faith that God would move through his absurd act of flinging a rock at a giant's head to slay Goliath.

There are an incredible number of Miracles recorded in the Old Testament during the prophetic ministries of Elijah and Elisha. These Miracles came through their Faith. One specific miracle came through an absurd act of Faith. Once Elijah had been taken up to heaven in a chariot of fire, Elisha inherited a double portion of Elijah's spirit and took on his anointing (*2 Kings 2:9-13*). Elisha went to Jericho afterward and it is there he is told the water is no good and the land is unproductive. Elisha's response is almost shocking, he tells the men to bring him a bowl of salt. It is almost the definition of absurd to toss salt into bitter waters. Salt has no inherit "water healing power." Elisha was acting in Faith to believe that the waters of Jericho and the land fed by that water would be restored by the power of God working through his absurd act.

These stories from Scripture prepare us to understand that nothing is too great for God to do and in fact, while people are never capable of pulling off the impossible, "*with God all things are possible (Matthew 19:26 NASB).*" It is my personal conviction that these absurd acts also remove the human ability to boast about what *they* did to affect this world. Instead, whatever they did is so laughable that only God can be given the glory.

Remember, the Gift of Faith was in operation in all of the Healings and Miracles of the New Testament church. The Acts of the Apostle's gives so many accounts of Healings and Miracles. Stephen was identified as having great faith: "*5...they did choose Stephen, a man full of faith and the Holy Spirit... 8And Stephen, full of faith and power, was doing great wonders and signs among the people (Acts 6:5b, 8 YLT)."* Philip's ministry was filled with the casting out of evil spirits and healing *(Acts 8:5-8)*. Paul was shipwrecked on his way to Rome and his statement in Acts 27, in the midst of his situation, is an excellent example of what the Gift of Faith looks like in circumstances that each of us may face in life. What Paul preached here is a principle of Faith that keeps us grounded even when we pray and don't see what we've asked for: *"So take heart, men, for I have faith in God that it will be exactly as I have been told (Acts 27:25 ESV)."*

The promises of God, pursuit of His will, and the application of Faith through prayers and actions will change this world. *"The effective prayer of a righteous man can accomplish much (James 5:16 NASB)."* James called to mind Genesis 15:6 where we are told that Abraham's Faith was counted to him as righteousness. Therefore, the prayer that James was talking about is one spoken in Faith that God *can* and trusting that He *will* accomplish what you're asking.

If you have the Faith that Jesus talked about in Matthew 17, the right kind of faith to affect this world, then whatever you say will happen. John does such an excellent job of repeating for us one more time that the prayers of Faith can have the power to change the world:

> *"¹⁴This is the confidence which we have before Him, that, if we ask anything according to His will, He hears us. ¹⁵And if we know that He hears us in whatever we ask, we know that we have the requests which we have asked from Him."*
> *1 John 5:14-15 NASB*

John identified one of the first hindrances in our asking and getting: did we pray in accordance with God's Will? Is what we prayed for in alignment with what we read in Scripture? Is it things that He has already promised? If it's not, then we need to reexamine what we are praying for and how we are asking. Accounts of believers and experiences of a post-Acts Church tell us that some times there are hindrances to Faith working in this world. We already know if it's not God's will, you can muster as much so-called faith as you would like, but God will not break His own order to things. There are several hindrances that require the attention of the Church and those praying in Faith that may be blocking how Faith can change our world.

Unfortunately, until Christ returns in Glory, this earth is under the control of Satan and his evil forces (*Luke 4:6* and *Ephesians 6:12*). Through demonic control, authority, and legal right, Faith may be limited in what it will accomplish. Please note: not what Faith *can* accomplish, because that is limitless, but what it *may* accomplish. There is a spirit that works in people to bring division between man and God through disobedience (*Ephesians 2:2*). The legal right of any demonic force is a contract—a claim, a license, or a permission—to remain and affect the outcomes in that person's life, if deliverance does not take place.

What things give demons legal rights? Sin, disobedience or rebellion, unforgiveness, curses (either generational or self-spoken), and any involvement in occult practices. This is a minor list, but we can trust that God has equipped His Church with members of each body to identify and minister to the unseen realm. The Gift of Words of Knowledge and the Gift of Discernings of Spirits will work together to bring to light any demonic stronghold that is preventing a word of Faith from being effective.

We must understand that our disobedience can cause our prayers to be fallow. Our disobedience separates us from God. If we continue in that disobedience without repentance, then any prayers we offer up to God are offensive to Him. We fail to keep His law, yet expect Him to do our bidding. David wrote in the Psalms, *"He who turns away his ear away from listening to the law [of God and man], Even his prayer is repulsive [to God] (Proverbs 28:9 AMP)."* John even clarified this for us in 1 John when he explained that those who are obedient to God receive answers to their prayers (*1 John 3:22*).

We know that sin separates us from God and if we are separated, then He does not hear. Isaiah wrote:

> *"But your iniquities have made a separation between you and your God, And your sins have hidden His face from you so that He does not hear." Isaiah 59:2 NASB*

It's not that God isn't actively listening to the prayers of believers, but it's such that our decision-making, our sin, separates us from His hearing. David understood this principle when he wrote about praising and worshipping God before presenting requests before God in prayer. David said:

> *"If I regard sin and baseness in my heart [that is, if I know it is there and do nothing about it], The Lord will not hear [me]." Psalm 66:18 AMP*

When the Gift of Faith is in operation, may it not be hindered by the sins of the ones praying or of the one receiving a Faith-filled prayer to effect his or her situation.

A great caution for all believers is how unforgiveness affects our prayers. In Matthew 5:21-24, Jesus was clear to instruct believers in the importance of settling issues between one another before coming to the altar of God to make offerings. We cannot justly petition God when our hearts are not right toward one of God's children. Jesus later impressed the importance of forgiving others when He said that God will forgive those who forgive and will not extend that same forgiveness to any who hold their brother's transgressions against them (*Matthew 6:14-15* and *Mark 11:25-26*).

The last hindrance to Faith I wish to address is doubt. This includes doubt from observers, doubt of the person receiving prayer, and, in some instances, the doubt of those praying. James gave instructions to the twelve tribes to pray in Faith:

> *"⁶But he must ask in faith without any doubting, for the one who doubts is like the surf of the sea, driven and tossed by the wind. ⁷For that man ought not to expect that he will receive anything from the Lord, ⁸being a double-minded man, unstable in all his ways." James 1:6-8* NASB

Doubt causes us to sink when Jesus is calling us to stand confidently. When Peter began to walk on the water he was doing it in Faith, but the moment he doubted was the moment that the supernatural power ceased to affect the world around Peter. Jesus made it clear that it was the doubting that affected Peter walking on water (*Matthew 14:31*).

As you begin to move in the Gift of Faith, do not allow the devil to bring discouragement, doubts, or accusations to you. Walk confidently that God is able to perform all according to His Will. Christ's sacrifice on the cross purchased your righteousness to be used by God to affect this world. Walk humbly with Him, submitting all to His Will. Tune your ear to what the Spirit says and the direction in which He is leading you to pray. See the world changed.

Healing
An Act of Fate or Faith?

"...and to another gifts of healings in the same Spirit;"
1 Corinthians 12:9b YLT

The topic of Healing seems to be growing increasingly controversial in today's modern Church. Influenced by culture and unable to reconcile the vast number of high profile Christians who do not experience Healing, the modern Church has found itself compromising the position and passion of the early Church on the topic of Healing. It would seem that today's Church has chalked up instances of God's supernatural Healing to mere chance or some kind of predestined fate that is unequally dispensed by God.

When I raise that question of whether Healing is an act of fate or faith I don't mean to trivialize it by any means. Is Healing something that comes to some and not to others based on chance? Some say that God and the Holy Spirit don't manifest supernaturally anymore. Some believe that modern medicine is God's answer to curing us from ailments and various diseases. I don't understand Healing, that's for sure, but I do believe that God heals. What's more is that I've seen it time and time again. I've seen Healing come through the manifestation of the Holy Spirit at work through members of the Church and a Gift of Healing. Healing is available. The question, it would seem, is how is it attainable?

The Apostle Paul wrote in his First Letter to the Church in Corinth Chapter 12 beginning in verse 4 of the nine Spiritual Gifts. When you read a literal translation of the original Greek, you find that what is often referred to as the Gift of Healing is actually "gifts of healings"—note the plurality here in both words.

Since I am not a Greek scholar, I choose to take Young's Literal Translation as being as literal to the English language as makes sense. This plurality indicates that there are multiple gifts to be used for the healing of various and certain sicknesses. In other words, wrapped up in this one Gift you have multiple gifts and multiple Healings. For example, an individual could receive, through the power of the Holy Spirit, the gift of healing for deafness. That is one gift or one occurrence of the healing of one type of sickness—deafness. This may be a temporary impartation of God's healing power. If, however, He consistently works through someone to heal many people of deafness, then He has imparted Gifts of Healing deafness.

The pluralities in both words indicate that God is consistently moving through an individual with multiple occurrences to heal many kinds of sicknesses. Paul operated in Gifts of Healings—through him healings occurred many different times and of many different sicknesses. Gifts of Healings are the manifestation of God's supernatural power against sickness. God's supernatural power enters into a person's body, drives out sickness and replaces it with health. His power is released through the believer with Gifts of Healings and received by the one who needs healing. The one with the Gift to impart the healing is a conduit, if you will, of God's Healing power.

When we pray for Healings we must be appropriating the Faith of God Himself to see Creation come back into alignment with the Creator's original intent. Remember, the Gift of Faith is about a deep, unwavering conviction and certainty in God's character. It is a deep-seated conviction that He continues to be who He said He is and who Scripture testifies He is. He *is* and it is because He is that supernatural Healings still happen. God Himself will impart to individuals Faith for certain types of Healing. Healing has been made available to followers of the one true God since Abraham. God is continuously faithful to the children of Abraham, Isaac, and Jacob when they cry out for Healing. David wrote throughout the Psalms that God heals sicknesses, illnesses, and diseases. Isaiah prophesied of a suffering servant, who we know to be Jesus, and proclaimed, "*by His scourging we are healed (Isaiah 53:5b NASB)*." The four Gospels and the Book of Acts are filled with examples of Healings through Faith. Rather than calling on God, Jesus spoke Healing directly into people.

We have that same authority to call Healing into bodies through the blood shed by Jesus on Calvary. We have that same authority to speak Healing into people. How do we know we have this authority? Because of the way Jesus sent out the seventy-two disciples in Luke Chapter 10 verse 9 to go into towns and heal the sick. Jesus expected His disciples to minister His Healing power to people. He commissioned them out, telling them to heal the sick. He imparted His Healing power to them to minister to people.

In Mark's account of Jesus sending out the Twelve Apostles, he said that they healed people through anointing the sick with oil (*Mark 6:13*). Peter and Paul both had Healings occur in their ministries. Peter and John went out to the temple and met a man unable to walk since birth. Peter said, "*In the name of Jesus Christ of Nazareth, rise up and walk (Acts 3:6 ESV)*!" He appropriated the authority of Jesus; Peter was given that authority by Jesus in Matthew 16:18. Paul saw Healing go out from his hands both through handkerchiefs he had touched and laying his hand on the sick (*Acts 19:11-12* and *28:8-9*). In fact, Acts 28:8 says that when Paul laid hands on the man, Paul healed him. Paul's Faith to see people healed released the

Healing power already given to him. Peter is abundantly clear on Pentecost that the Baptism of the Holy Spirit, and by extension all the Gifts of the Holy Spirit, will be available to "...*all who are far off, as many as the Lord our God will call to Himself (Acts 2:39 NASB)*." I believe this means that we as Christians living in the Twenty-first Century have the same authority as Peter and Paul had as Christians living in the First Century.

I've heard people ask, "Well, doesn't God love people enough to heal them if we just ask?" I understand the place in our hearts that question comes from, but I don't believe it's the right question. He Loves us more than we can ever *know*, literally Know. Ephesians 3:17-19 clearly states that our understanding of His Love for us is inextricably linked to our faith. Of course there are numerous testimonies of people being healed as they are asking alone. I think this is the question to ask: are we asking for Healing because of some deontological sense of "faith," some rote commitment to our religion like religious duty, or are we really asking Him for Healing? Are we asking because any "good" Christian should ask God to heal them?

Only He can judge the faith we muster together and apply to our prayers. I believe this to be true though: True Faith yields breakthrough in our lives. It is often that through the Gifts of Healings paired with Faith in prayer and the faith of those coming to receive that Healing takes place. This is not always the case and it does deserve an examination. There are two hindrances to receiving Healing that can be linked together here: a lack of knowledge about Healing in general (or even its availability) and unbelief. Healing comes by Faith.

People tend to immediately go on the offense when their faith for Healing is brought into question. Raising the question is not meant to condemn, but rather to bring focus where clarity is needed. One account after another in the Gospels attribute peoples' Healings to their faith individually and sometimes to the faith of people who cared for them. Quick examples for the faith of other believers are the centurion's servant (*Luke 7:1-10*), the paralytic lowered through the roof (*Luke 5:17-39*), and the demon possessed daughter of the Canaanite woman (*Matthew 15:21-28*).

Other places throughout the Gospels indicate that the Faith of individuals in Jesus Christ as Lord is what sets Healing into motion. Jesus was frequently quoted to say that one's faith had healed them or made them well. The woman with the issue of blood had Faith to believe if she could simply touch a piece of cloth, which Jesus was wearing, His power could bring her Healing (*Luke 8:43-48*). Luke 18:35-43 gives an account of Jesus healing a blind beggar with no indication of physical contact from Jesus.

Faith is powerful. From Jesus physically laying hands on people to not even being in the same town as the sick person, Healing is recorded throughout the Gospels. Most importantly, there is no record in Scripture of Jesus explicitly denying someone Healing. He never said that their sickness was too far along, too severe, or most importantly that it was not the Will of the Father to heal them. Obviously, Jesus did not come and heal every sick or afflicted person wherever he traveled. Scripture does explain that He was limited in performing miracles in His hometown of Nazareth, but was able to heal some (*Matthew 13:53-58* and *Mark 6:1-5*). Matthew and Mark both attribute this to the unbelief of the people there.

Christ must have left some towns before every sick person was healed. We need to remember that His purpose for coming to this world was to bring us salvation from the sickness of the soul—sin and eternal separation from the Father. For any sick or afflicted person left in those towns, when the disciples received the Baptism of the Holy Spirit they were equipped to minister Healing to them. Christ promised, "...*whoever believes in me will also do the works that I do; and greater works than these will he do... (John 14:12 ESV).*"

Apply the Faith to know that God's character is to heal those who believe in Him and love His Son. The Gift of Healing in operation is not merely an act of predetermined fate of Healing, but it is the work of faith in and through believers in Christ. That means now. Healing is for now on this earth. Do not limit God to some warm and fuzzy religious idea that "well, we're all healed in heaven when we get our glorified bodies." Is that enough for you? God says Healing is available to us now, in this body, on this earth as evidenced in Scripture.

Knowing what the Word of God says about Healing addresses both the hindrances of a lack of knowledge and unbelief. It is incredibly faith building to read of the numerous Healings in the Old and New Testaments with all of their varying circumstances and severities. The occasion of being healed by God is not a matter of His Will. He already willed it; Isaiah received revelation of this and Peter experienced it (*Isaiah 53:4-5* and *1 Peter 2:24*). God has already established access to His Healing power through the death of Jesus on the cross. It is a matter of us understanding how to appropriate that Healing in our lives.

People say, "Well, I've seen people pray for healing with a lot of faith and people still die from their diseases. So, why did God let them die if they were believing for healing?" I do not understand the providence of God. All I Know is that Jesus attributed Healing to Faith at an incredibly reliable rate to hold a Scripturally sound understanding that Healing comes from Faith. But once again, I think it's the wrong question to ask. The question to ask is: what else were you missing while you were praying? Again, this isn't meant to be condemnatory; it is intended to be a challenge to your preconceptions of Faith and God's character. Our natural man wants to reject this notion, but is the person who needs healing harboring resentment and unforgiveness toward anyone? Are there sins that have gone unconfessed or unrepented for to God? Have they ever been involved in occult practices? Have they in any way worshipped or sought out spiritual "counsel" from sources other than the Holy Spirit? Have they made covenant with any one person, group, or god other than Yahweh?

God promised that those who serve Him wholly and only will be blessed and said, "*I will remove sickness from your midst... I will fulfill the number of your days (Exodus 23:25b, 26b NASB)*." When ministering God's Gift of Healing to someone encourage him or her to ask the Lord for forgiveness, repent, and renounce his or her involvement in the things listed above. These things can be barriers to receiving Healing.

There are other instructions given by Jesus and Paul when praying for healing. Jesus as our example leads us to lay hands on the sick when praying for healing (a few include: *Mark 6:5, Mark 7:32-33, Luke 13:13*). He then promised to those who believe that when they lay hands on the sick they will be healed (*Mark 16:17-18*). We have access to God's Healing power through faith in Jesus Christ because He promised us that we will do the same works He did on Earth and more as representatives of Him as He sits at the right-hand of the Father in Heaven (*John 14:12*).

This leads us to another important piece of understanding that is critical to see Healing: authority. We must understand from where our authority to pray for, receive, and see Healing take place comes. You can't merely call on the name of Jesus. You must be a son or daughter of Christ in order to use His name with the authority to receive Healing. If you are ministering to someone through the Gift of Healing, you should start by asking him or her about his or her relationship with Jesus. Faith activates Healing. It is the catalyst to initiate acts of reaching out to receive a healing. Since Faith is *"the assurance of things hoped for, and the conviction of things not seen (Hebrews 11:2 NASB),"* it is how we trust that Jesus' death and resurrection purchased our righteousness or right standing with God. It is this right standing with our Creator that gives us access to the throne of grace to ask for Healing and it is this right standing with God that allows us to call down Healing into others (*Hebrews 10:19-21 HCSB*).

We also see evidence of Healing by the laying on of hands in Paul's ministry (*Acts 28:8-9*). Paul gave several other instructions and examples of essential faith elements necessary to see Healing take place. In James 5:14-15, Paul instructed that if anyone is sick he should go to the elders of the church and they should anoint him with oil in the name of the Lord and pray over him. Through this Scripture and Mark 6:13, we can understand that through anointing the sick with oil and laying hands on them, God's Healing power can be channeled through believers to those who are sick.

This brings us back to understanding authority, but we must also understand and respect God's anointing and those He has anointed and to whom He has given Spiritual Gifts of Healings. This takes us to Acts 19:11-12 where an account is given of Healing coming through the anointing of items by those who are anointed to be used for Healing. So, the laying on of hands is good if you are able to, but there is also a transference that can take place that can carry Healing through a physical object.

The power of God can also fall so heavily in a place, a physical space, that it can permeate it and charge it with supernatural power for people to receive Healing. This biblical truth can be found in John 5:2-4 NASB:

> "*2Now there is in Jerusalem by the sheep gate a pool, which is called in Hebrew Bethesda, having five porticoes. 3In these lay a multitude of those who were sick, blind, lame, and withered, [waiting for the moving of the waters; 4for an angel of the Lord went down at certain seasons into the pool and stirred up the water; whoever then first, after the stirring up of the water, stepped in was made well from whatever disease with which he was afflicted.]*"

As the angel stirred up the waters, God's Healing power permeated the pool and healed the person from whatever ailment they once suffered.

Luke wrote an account where Jesus was teaching in a place with Pharisees and law professors present when the paralytic man was lowered through the roof by his friends. When you read Luke 5:17 in the New American Standard Bible translation, it says, "*...the power of the Lord was <u>present</u> for Him to perform healing.*" This is genuinely incredible and both are wonderful examples of God's tradition of meeting people for healing in a place. What is even more incredible is that as Christ ascended to heaven He sent the Holy Spirit to be with us as the Helper to accomplish things in His name (*John 14:18-26*).

The Holy Spirit dwells with us and in us as we receive the Baptism of the Holy Spirit and where we go we take Him with us to perform Healings, Miracles, and good works in the name of Jesus. We see this in Peter's ministry a little after the Day of Pentecost. As Peter received the Baptism of the Holy Spirit, he carried with him the power of the Holy Spirit to heal people. Peter's own shadow was supernaturally charged with Healing power, so much so that when his shadow passed over the sick as he walked out of the city people were healed (*Acts 5:15-16*).

We need to be careful not to judge why someone does not receive a healing. I urge particular caution in judging the faith of the individual. However, the Bible does indicate that doubt, unbelief, or a lack of faith can be a barrier to receive Healing. That's hard to understand and our heart, mind, and soul all struggle with that notion. There is a difference, I believe, between a doubter and a Christian who is struggling with momentary doubt or temporary unbelief. Again, I urge you not to judge the individuals, but Scripture says to ask in faith without doubting. I understand this to mean: "within the context of faith, from the place of believing in Christ, do not ask with skepticism." A warning against doubting, to be sure. It may be a weakness for them in their own sickness that allows doubt to creep in. In some cases I don't consider this kind of doubt to be doubting that He *can*, I think it is more a doubting that He *will*. As individuals receive Gifts of Healings to impart God's Healing power to others, they must activate their own faith and I would encourage them to intercede for the faith of the person who needs healing.

The barriers to healing that I've addressed above are those that come about through our own actions, whether we were aware of the consequences they would bear or not. Paul also included a vital aspect of Healing, which is confession, repentance, and the forgiveness of sins. We should desire to be clean before the Lord, repenting for any sin that may prevent us from receiving Healing. If there is a lack of knowledge, unbelief, unforgiveness, unrepentance, or involvement with other spiritual powers we can identify these things, turn from them, and consciously pursue more of Christ in replacing the influence these things have on us.

There is another barrier that must be addressed: the sickness itself or the barrier to Healing may be the effect of a curse. I place no limit on the ways in which a curse comes upon a person, but I do want to specifically address a particular kind of curse: the generational curse. In Exodus 20, God said that the sins of a father will follow through to his children even to the fourth generation. The disciples understood this to mean that the sins of parents could bear curses down upon their children (*John 9:1-3*), specifically with respect to Healing.

It is important to note that in this Biblical example, Jesus denied that it was a generational curse, but He does not rebuke the notion of a generational curse. If generational curses were a misconception of Exodus 20, or would be wiped away for believers, this would be a perfect opportunity for Jesus to address it and a record be made. Instead, I believe Jesus is encouraging us to discern and not to judge *why* Healing is needed. If you believe that you may be under a generational curse and it is blocking your Healing, I encourage you to break that curse over you and the generations to follow you. How do you break a curse? You claim the blood of Christ's power over you, having purchased you from sin's chains, and renounce any legal claim the devil may have over you because of the sins of your parents and grand-parents going back four generations.

I believe there is one more barrier that exists that must be dealt with properly: Demonic oppression. This can be a barrier to Healing by being the cause of the sickness, disease, malady, etc., through a spirit of infirmity. Luke 13:11-12 is the account of a woman with an evil spirit of infirmity causing her affliction. The Amplified version gives great insight into the language here. When Jesus rebuked the infirmity— effectively calling for deliverance—and laid hands on her, she was released from the demonic oppression causing a physical malady and she was healed. If she had not first been delivered from the spirit of infirmity, then praying directly for her back to be straightened would not have addressed the root problem. That is not to say that she necessarily would not have been healed, but that evil spirit would have still been present and capable of wreaking havoc later. Mark 9:14-29 tells the story of a young boy who is afflicted by demonic spirits causing, among many other things, muteness and deafness. Jesus explained that some demonic spirits of infirmity only come out by prayer and fasting.

This also leads us to claiming and keeping the healing for which we've asked God. Sometimes Healing is gradual. If you have asked God for Healing and received prayer for Healing in accordance with Scripture a lot also depends on how you respond. Just because you walk away and don't "feel" healed doesn't mean Jesus didn't give you Healing for your sickness. Continue to claim the healing and receive it in spite of how you feel.

Understand that God in His omnipotence is working His Healing power in you and may also be working to reveal more of His Word and character as part of a holistic healing process. There is power in praising God. Praising Him reclaims His glory in our lives by redirecting our focus back to His goodness. Thank God for His Healing power, Christ's sacrifice which purchased it, and continue to proclaim Healing. If symptoms of sickness reappear, it does not mean that you were not healed. To be sure, Satan is a liar, who schemes and deceives the people of God to convince them that they have not properly heard or understood God. The devil comes to steal the gifts and promises God has given us.

It is important to understand that the Spiritual Gifts are critical for the Church. Paul lists Faith and Healing in tandem to one another. They are tethered to each other. Of course, Paul continued to write about the key role that each member of the Church body has in using these Gifts. They are meant to encourage one another. So, when praying for Healing it would be prudent to have a) the Holy Spirit ushered in and welcomed, and b) to invite the Holy Spirit to manifest His awesome power through individuals to whom He has given Gifts of wonder working Faith, extraordinary powers of Healing, and the Working of Miracles. To have one who is anointed for Healing, Faith, and Miracles all in one or in many people is an incredible ministry, but we should not forsake he or she who Discerns Between the Spirits.

Discerning of Spirits is what allowed Jesus to identify that the woman and the boy both needed deliverance from an evil spirit before they could receive Healing. As you begin to operate in a Gift of Healing, humble yourself, submit to the leading and sensitivity of the Holy Spirit, release faith and believe that God has anointed you to impart His Healing power into the bodies of the sick. Remember, God is responsible for the outcome and its timing. You are responsible to be faithful to step out in the Gift He has given you and to obey the instructions for Healing laid out in Scripture.

Miracles
Magic or Magnificence?

"and to another in-workings of mighty deeds..."
1 Corinthians 12:10a YLT

The word for "miracles" can also be translated as "mighty deeds." Miracles are certainly "mighty deeds" and, as the original Greek describes, this Gift is similar to Healings in that the effecting or the in-workings are plural. So, just like Gifts of Healings, the Effecting of Miracles is uniquely identified by multiple manifestations of the Gift with every individual miracle.

Miracles are quite literally the manifested power of God through the Holy Spirit and only under the direction of God Almighty. We do not get to choose what Miracles God performs and when. Having the Gift of the Effecting of Miracles is not like working magic. Miracles are not performed through spell casting. They are performed through the Magnificence of God as an extension of His mighty deeds over Creation. We are merely an instrument of Faith to be used by God as a conduit for His power over everything.

Miracles are a separate display of God's supernatural power from Healings. While these two manifestations of God's power often seem to overlap or coincide, there are some helpful distinctions to make between the two. These distinctions are important to understand because when you pray you should pray with such specific purpose that your prayer is effective. Healings are directed specifically to the replacing of sickness or disease with health. Sometimes Healings happen slowly, but not without the presence of God's Healing touch. Many times Healings happen internally and are unseen by the natural eye and without the aid of science.

Miracles are more frequently instantaneous and seen in some way—in a naturally measurable way. While Healings replace sickness with health, Miracles will restore something that was lost, remove something that shouldn't be there, or create something that was missing entirely. Faith plays a critical role in the effectiveness of prayers for Healings and Miracles, but Miracles are directly attached to acts of Faith. Some Miracles are also Healings, but not all Healings would be considered Miracles under this distinction. However, we understand that we commonly use the word "miracle" when referring to supernatural intervention. Still, the Gifts of Healings and the Gifts of the Effecting of Miracles are listed separately and therefore must be unique phenomena.

A command of Faith can release the Miracle working power of God. It may still take the faith of the receiver to believe that God can or at the very least an openness to the possibility, but the Faith of the one ministering can impart faith to the receiver. Sometimes we may need to prompt the faith of the receiver. This can be done through audibly expressing our own Faith that God will, if only the receiver accepts, believes, and receives, or through an act of Faith that encourages the faith of the receiver.

We can take hold of the promise of Miracles through Faith when we mix the Word of God with Faith. The power of the Word has not changed. It is both living and active, therefore proclaiming Scriptures' promise of God's ability to work Miracles will have the same effect now as it did when it was first spoken by the Holy Spirit. Miracles release the full and awesome power of God into a situation. His power and His authority demand an instantaneous response from Creation. Just as we discussed with a word of Faith spoken in authority, when and where such words are spoken Miracles happen. God provides the Gift and the power through the Spirit to work Miracles by hearing with Faith.

Paul wrote to the Galatians a rebuke to remind them that God works Miracles by hearing with faith. He reminded them that they received the Spirit by faith and so Miracles come about through Faith (*Galatians 3:1-5*). Paul believed that God equips each congregation with at least one person to exercise the Effecting of Miracles and impart faith through Faith for others to receive the Spirit (*1 Corinthians 12:28*). His point was the Faith of some believers can have a profound impact on the faith of other believers. Paul continually pointed out the importance of these Gifts to the life of the Church when he stated that true apostles perform "*signs and wonders and miracles (2 Corinthians 12:12b NASB)*." The Gifts of Miracles are not limited to a special select number of Christians. The Gifts arise from the Baptism of the Holy Spirit and are available to all believers.

Miracles go further than Healings. They are released by an action of Faith, even an absurd act of Faith. Scripture shows us many examples that when Miracles happen they are usually the direct result of words of Faith matched with acts of Faith—absurd acts—that release the Miracle. The Holy Spirit alone must inspire these acts. Although we would commonly say the woman with the issue of blood was healed from her condition, it was actually a Miracle. The Gospel accounts make it clear that her condition was not a curable sickness. She had spent all her money on doctors and had actually ended up worse. She needed a Miracle—a restoration of proper function in her body—and by Faith she reached out and received one. Her action was absurd. How could simply touching the hem of His garment heal her?! Her Faith reached out, touched Him and she grabbed ahold of a Miracle for herself (*Mark 5:25-34* and *Luke 8:43-48*).

It is under the direction of the Holy Spirit that these acts can bring about the Effecting of Miracles, not just because it is through His Baptism that power is imparted, but also because it was the Holy Spirit that brooded over the void to prepare for the effecting of Creation into existence. Scripture says that God was preparing Creation and the Holy Spirit was hovering, fluttering, moving over the water to bring about God's creation (*Genesis 1:1-2 HCSB, YLT, NASB*). The Holy Spirit works to bring about God's Will on this Earth. Inspired acts of the Holy Spirit are never formulaic solutions. They are inspired in such a way that no credit can be attributed to the wit, natural wisdom, or knowledge of the persons involved.

The life of Abraham has so much to teach us about the Christian walk, faith in God, the faith *of* God, and God's work to intervene in our lives when we are willing to submit to His Spirit and His Will. I would be remiss if I did not mention the miracle of Isaac's conception and birth. Jehovah Himself appeared to Abraham and promised that in one year's time Sarah would have a son (*Genesis 18:1, 10 YLT*). As we read in Genesis 18:11 it is revealed that Sarah was old and well past the time for a woman to bear children. The promise itself was absurd, yet Jehovah spoke the word with the same authority as He did at Creation. Despite the unbelief of Sarah and the struggling will of Abraham to hold on to the promise, God was faithful to affect a Miracle in Sarah's womb. Jehovah restored Sarah's womb to conceive a child and then created a life within her womb. This confirms the faithfulness of God to perform Miracles throughout all of Scripture.

Throughout the Old Testament God consistently favored the Hebrews in battle. They won against all odds, yet one particular battle speaks to the Miracle working power of God as we've defined—a work that effects Creation. Joshua requested of God and spoke with a word of Faith that time stand still to give Israel the advantage. Joshua 10:13 says, "*And the sun stopped in the middle of the sky and did not hasten to go down for about a whole day (NASB)*." Joshua's word of Faith, spoken with the authority of leadership given to him by God, had the power to affect the rising and the setting of the sun. "*There was no day like that before it or after it, when the Lord listened to the voice of a man; for the Lord fought for Israel (Joshua 10:14 NASB)*." This is the Effecting of Miracles that the God of Israel would hear the plea of a man to effect a situation in alignment with God's Will.

The Miracles of God performed before Christ's presence on this earth are such a wonderful reminder of God's faithfulness to His people. These Miracles attest to God's affection for those that love Him. When the children of Israel were taken captive by Babylon, three young men carved out a place in the King's court. Shadrach, Meshach, and Abednego were faced with a life and death decision. This Sunday School story is well known by many believers. Yet, there are two things that make this story more than a tale of what happens when you refuse to worship false gods and stand up to worship the one true God. The first is a word of authority spoken in Faith. These three young men faced King Nebuchadnezzar and confidently proclaimed that their God was more powerful to affect this world than the king himself:

> "*17If it be so, our God whom we serve is able to deliver us from the furnace of blazing fire; and He will deliver us out of your hand, O king. 18But even if He does not, let it be known to you, O king, that we are not*

going to serve your gods or worship the
golden image that you have set up."
Daniel 3:17-18 NASB

The men ended with an important contingency: they were wholly submitted to the unknown Will of God. They gave themselves over to the possibility that God would not deliver them from the burning furnace. They believed He could, they believed He would, but they submitted themselves to the notion that they could be wrong, not out of doubt, but out of humility. When these men were finally thrown into the furnace, the king's warriors were instantly killed by the fire. Not only were Shadrach, Meshach, and Abednego not instantly killed, but lo and behold, they were joined in the furnace by an angel to save them. The men were released without the smell of smoke on them and they attributed their deliverance to their Faith that God could affect this world. It was a Miracle.

When we have Faith to believe for a Miracle, conviction of God's ability to work it, we must also submit to His greater Will and plan. The Miracles of the Old Testament teach us this principle well. The men and women of great Faith in the Old Testament were wholly submitted to God's will, even unto death. They also mixed their private faith with absurd acts of Faith and saw God intervene. When praying for a Miracle we must be submitted to the unknown plan of God to accomplish His greater Will for humanity. What I mean to say is that we do not get the privilege of deciding what Miracles occur when. However, this Gift of the Effecting of Miracles is the Gift to work a mighty deed—a wonder-filled event—beyond man's natural ability, which displays God's supernatural power over Creation and fulfills only His Will and purpose. Those with the Gift of the Effecting of Miracles must be incredibly sensitive to His Will and purpose when praying for or proclaiming the working of a Miracle.

There are several accounts of the blind receiving sight throughout Scripture. All of these accounts are Healings, but one is described with a particular detail that indicates Jesus performed a Miracle of sight. In John Chapter 9 Jesus encountered a man born blind sitting outside of the temple begging. Jesus spit in the dirt, made clay, and rubbed it on the man's eyes (*John 9:6*). This is clearly an inspired act of the Holy Spirit. Why do I say this is inspired? Clay is the medium of Creation used by God (*Genesis 2:7*, *Job 10:9*, *Job 33:6*). Jesus creatively made a man born blind see. This Scripture is clear that it was not a slowly degenerating eye disease, but that the man had actually never been able to see. His eyes never functioned the way eyes were intended at Creation to function. Inspired by the Holy Spirit, Jesus mixed together the element of Creation and restored that man's eyes to see. Is it possible that the man had even been born without eyes at all and Jesus created them out of the dust? This example shows us that while this man was healed of his blindness, he needed a Miracle to see.

In Luke we read an account of ten lepers who were healed of their leprosy, but just like the blind man, there is more than a Miracle at work there. Jesus entered a particular village on His way to Jerusalem. The leprous men cried out to Jesus for mercy. Jesus' instructions were for the men to go to the priests. The men responded in obedient faith and went out toward the temple. Luke 17:14b AMP says, "*And as they went, they were [miraculously] healed and made clean.*" The leprosy immediately disappeared with their faith-filled response to Jesus' directions. Since they were declared "unclean" by law, it was illegal for them to go into the temple and therefore, to see the priests while still unclean (*Leviticus 13 & 14*). Yet, they believed Christ's words. It is an absurd act to do exactly what you are not suppose to do and yet, it is inspired by the Holy Spirit because it activated their faith to believe for and receive a Miracle in their bodies.

This passage touches on another important aspect of receiving Miracles (and Healings), which is the importance of continuous praise to God for His Miraculous power working in your life. Only one of the ten turned back to praise God for what He had done. Jesus said to the man, "*Get up and go [on your way]. Your faith [your personal trust in Me and your confidence in God's power] has restored you to health (Luke 17:19 AMP).*" God is seeking those who minds and hearts are set on the worship and glory of Him only.

The Book of Acts is filled with numerous accounts of Healings and Miracles. Absurd acts are committed under the belief that in spite of their ridiculousness, God will move through it, and therefore only He will receive the praise. As Christ's apostles, Peter and John had witnessed Christ's miracle working power directly and saw Jesus continually point to the Father. They took Jesus' words to heart when He said, "*Whatever you ask in My name, that will I do, so that the Father may be glorified in the Son (John 14:13 NASB).*"

Peter and John encountered a man born crippled begging at the gate of the temple called Beautiful. Peter told the man they had no money to give him, but instead proclaimed a word of authority, "*in the name of Jesus Christ of Nazareth, rise up and be walking (Acts 3:6 YLT).*" As Peter made this bold statement he grabbed the man by his right hand, pulled him to his feet releasing God's power into his body through an act of Faith. Immediately strength, which had never been present, surged through this man's legs, ankles, and feet. He leaped upright, standing for the first time, and began to walk. His walking turned to leaping and praising God as he entered the temple.

Peter necessarily had to be under the direction and inspiration of the Holy Spirit to pull a man born lame to his feet. It is absurd to believe that a man whose bones and muscles had never been able to hold him upright would suddenly be able to do so simply by pulling him up to stand. However, under the inspiration of the Holy Spirit such an act of authoritative Faith, spoken in the name of Christ, will have the effectiveness to cause a lame man to stand and spontaneously support himself. Only the inspiration of the Holy Spirit to commit such an absurd act of Faith could affect a Miracle for a man to stand, walk, and leap immediately.

Although Miracles may be so obviously supernatural, not all Miracles are created equal. Some Miracles are described as extraordinary. In Acts 19:11 Luke wrote, "*God was performing extraordinary miracles by the hands of Paul (NASB)*." The Young's Literal Translation describes these Miracles as "not common," so there must have been what was considered common Miracles and then some Miracles that were unusual (*Acts 19:11 AMP*). Since Miracles are the direct manifestation of God's magnificence it is no wonder at all that some Miracles are extraordinary. Miracles are beyond what magic, sorcery, or the conjuring of tricks can manage to effect. In fact, in Acts it is made clear that Miracles are not magic as those that practiced magic burned their books when they saw these Miracles as a manifestation of God's magnificence (*Acts 19:17b-19*).

God is still performing Miracles. Scripture declares, "*Jesus Christ is the same yesterday and today and forever (Hebrews 13:8 NASB)*." God does not change, His Kingdom has no end (*Luke 1:30-33*), and He teaches us to pray that what His Will is in Heaven so will it also be on earth (*Matthew 6:10*). When we mix together these Scriptures with Faith to believe that we can actually call Heaven down to earth, we can understand that the perfection of Heaven can be manifested here on earth now. Miracles are available to us. Just as with Healing there is an authority granted to believers through the blood shed by Christ on the cross. The Psalmist pondered and the writer of Hebrews reiterated that God has given man authority over this world.

> *"⁴What is man that You take thought of him, And the son of man that You care for him?... ⁶You make him to rule over the works of Your hands; You have put all things under his feet..."Psalm 8:4 & 6 NASB*

He has given the faithful the power of the Holy Spirit to affect this world. Through signs, wonders, miracles, and by the Gifts of the Holy Spirit poured out after Pentecost, God confirms His offer of salvation. The Workings of Miracles is not for the glory of anyone but God Himself.

Faith, Healings, and Miracles are sensitive topics. We can, in our enthusiasm to see God manifested, push people too hard. We must learn the prompting of the Holy Spirit when ministering Healings and Miracles. We cannot use formulas. We cannot simply say, "Well, Peter just pulled a man to his feet, so let me yank a wheelchair out from under a man."

We are conveying the power of God to people and how He reaches them and touches them is uniquely up to the Holy Spirit. Be led by Him alone. It may look like something you've read in Scripture before or it may look nothing like that. Be encouraged by the numerous accounts of Miracles throughout the Bible. When stepping out in this Gift it is important to have the compassion of Christ for the person in need of a Miracle. Jesus saw these people as held back and bound by the work of Satan to restrict them from fulfilling God's purpose for their lives. We need to be as filled with love for the person in need as we are filled with a passion that burns against the wickedness of the Enemy's plans for their life.

Remember that our faith is built up by the Word of God, because, "*faith comes from hearing, and hearing by the word of Christ (Romans 10:17 NASB)*." As the Church continues to step out and move in the Gifts of the Holy Spirit as the Early Church did in the generation of Pentecost, so we as individuals need to be familiar with what Scripture promises about Miracles. It is the Bible that will continue to be effective on the conditions of this world, because it is by the Word of God that Creation came into existence and it is by the Word of God that it will return to its original intended operation.

Paul wrote to one of the churches that the Word can possess and dwell inside us and bring encouragement to one another "*with all wisdom teaching and admonishing one another with psalms and hymns and spiritual songs... (Colossians 3:16 NASB)*." When we are ministering to one another and even to non-Christians the gift of salvation through signs and wonders, such as Healings and Miracles, we must approach with love in our hearts for that person. We must know the Word of God so that we can administer the Word of God. This is not to bring condemnation, but to apply the Miracle-working balm of Gilead. Miracles are not magic tricks we are performing. They are the direct, intentional, and personal manifest presence of God intervening in our lives on this earth.

Prophecy
Fortune Telling or
Father's Revelation?

"and to another prophecy..."
1 Corinthians 12:10b NASB

There seems to be some confusion among Christians about the Gift of Prophecy—what it is, its purpose, and its boundaries. From as early as the accounts in Genesis to the last chapter of the book of Revelation, God used prophetic words and prophets to speak to His people. God continues to use the Gift of Prophecy to attract the attention of the Church to listen to what the Spirit of God is saying and the direction He is giving. We should be careful not to mistake prophecy for mere fortune telling or mystical speculations about the future. Prophecy as a Gift of the Holy Spirit is to be used to provoke individuals to examine in greater depth God's promises to His people.

Prophecy tends to be popularly thought of as more mystical, or magical even, then some of the other Gifts. There is skepticism about the legitimacy of prophecy or even whether such a Gift is in operation today. As we approach the period of the End Times and the Second Coming of Christ, the Church most certainly needs the supernatural and divine direction of God. The Gift of Prophecy was not just for the Church in Corinth. It was poured out on the day of Pentecost for any Spirit-filled believer who so desired to be used by God in that way. Peter reminded the crowd in Acts 2 of Joel's prophecy for the End Times (*Joel 2:28-29*):

> *"[17]'And it shall be in the last days,' God says, '...your sons and your daughters shall prophesy... [18]Even on my bondslaves, both*

> *men and women, I will in those days pour*
> *forth of My spirit And they shall prophesy."*
> *Acts 2:17-18 NASB*

We have not seen the rest of Joel 2 come to pass. That prophetic word means there is still a time coming and the Gift of Prophecy will still be in operation in His Church out of necessity. All can prophesy. It is not a Gift of favoritism or speciality. It is not given only to the most holy, righteous, or "spiritual" of Christian believers. Paul told the Corinthians, "*For you can all prophesy one by one, so that everyone may learn and everyone may be encouraged (1 Corinthians 14:31 HCSB)."*

Similar to a Word of Knowledge or a Word of Wisdom, a Prophecy will not emerge out of an person's own knowledge—education or understanding—or from their own wisdom applied to the situation. Like the other Gifts, Prophecy is given only through the supernatural power of the Holy Spirit to a Believer. True Prophecy is a direct revelation from God—words from God that impart counsel, reveal His purposes, and bring encouragement to His people about the direction and plan He has for them.

The Gift of Prophecy works through a Believer as a mouthpiece or conduit for God's words of guidance and intentions for an individual, His Church, a generation, or even a nation. Paul said in 1 Corinthians 14:1 that we should seriously desire the Gifts of the Holy Spirit and the Gift of Prophecy most of all. But why? Well, I believe the "why" is found in the beauty of the purpose of Prophecy. God is looking for a Church—a Bride—that speaks life into a dying world. God wants to speak through us to other people and He does that through the prophetic.

The 14th chapter of First Corinthians focuses on the Gift of Prophecy. It is here that Paul gives a great amount of instruction to the Church regarding this Gift. The Gift of Prophecy is used in order to edify—instruct and uplift—the Church. Prophecy is not just for edification, but for exhortation (correction or caution) and consolation (comfort). The benefit of Prophecy to the Church is to enlighten, encourage, and excite it to fulfill its purpose in God's plan. Since Paul encouraged all to desire the Gift of Prophecy it is also important to understand what it is not and how it is not to be used. Beyond these three purposes, prophecy cannot be true prophecy and it would then only be used for the benefit of whoever is speaking rather than for the whole Church. The Gift of Prophecy is not given only to special Christians; if it were, why then would Paul encourage everyone to desire it?!

We are baptized *into* the Holy Spirit and the Spirit, Scripture says, dwells deep within us (*1 Corinthians 3:16*). We can then draw from the Spirit like a well of the living water Christ promised to all believers in John 7:37-39. Prophecy comes as living water bubbling from the well of our spirit to minister revelation of what God is speaking in a particular situation. The Gift of Prophecy now functions as revelation perceived. In other words, what the Spirit of God is saying through someone with a Gift of Prophecy will naturally be filtered and presented through the lens of that individuals' experiences, education, personality, and unique command of language. For this reason, it would be prudent to preface any supposed prophetic word with saying, "I perceive..." or "I believe the Lord is saying..." rather than a definitive "Thus says the Lord." Likewise, for those judging the prophecy rightly as directed there should be consideration and grace given due to this seemingly natural disposition.

Prophecy reveals the heart of God the Father for His Children. It is a revelation of His plans and purposes for those to whom He is speaking. A prophetic word can also initiate a blessing over the future life of the one receiving the prophecy. For example, both Isaac and Jacob bless their sons and these birthright blessings prophetically launch the destiny of a nation. Isaac's blessing of Jacob, who is later renamed Israel from whom all Jewish people derive their ancestry, established Israel's future claims on the Promised Land and its importance in human history. The blessing ends with *"cursed be everyone who curses you, and blessed be everyone who blesses you (Genesis 27:27-29 ESV)."* Israel has risen and fallen throughout the course of history, but it is still true that blessings come to nations that stand with Israel. When Jacob gathered his sons the blessing he spoke over Judah became a prophetic release of promise over that tribe—the tribe from which King David and Jesus came (*Genesis 49:8-12*).

The Old Testament is filled with prophecies about the rise and fall of Israel, the coming Savior, and the End Times. While Prophecy is used here to bring correction to Israel for its adulterous worship of false gods, it is also used to remind Israel that favor and blessing will return to the nation when it turns back to worshipping God and follows His commandments. From the major to the minor prophets, the theme of Prophecy is God's purpose and promise for His people. Although there are many Biblical prophecies about the End Times, which have not yet come to pass, we can see through Isaiah, Jeremiah, Ezekiel and more that prophecies can be a warning of things to come if God's people do not turn from their wicked ways. Biblical prophetic words about the rise and fall of nations have all been true and those with timelines have fallen exactly within the time period God said it would. It is important to remember the purpose of prophecy and not to treat it as divining the future or mere uncanny coincidence.

When remembering the purpose of Prophecy, being mindful of what it is not, we must understand that all Prophecy is open to judgement. As we further examine the Old Testament we see that God gives Moses instructions for judging a prophet:

> *"21You may say in your heart, 'How will we know the word which the Lord has not spoken?' 22When a prophet speaks in the name of the Lord, if the thing does not come about or come true, that is the thing which the Lord has not spoken. The prophet has spoken it presumptuously..."*
> *Deuteronomy 18:21-22 NASB*

Those with the Gift of Prophecy must remain humble. He or she cannot be captivated by thoughts of self-importance. They must remain mindful that they are one of many parts of the Body of Christ with all parts working together (*1 Corinthians 12:12-27*). A prophet is not to be established as the sole conveyor of God's purpose and promise to others. A prophet should not march around a Church barking orders at the leadership or proclaiming whimsical life advice to the people around them. The Gift is for the building up of the Church to become the Bride of Christ, not to govern the Church as a person to be feared. Humility should rule the heart of the prophet.

Paul wrote to the Church in Corinth that in church meetings prophetic words should be evaluated or discerned for truthfulness (*1 Corinthians 14:29*). Since there were known to be false prophets, John encouraged the Church to test the spirit working behind the words of a so-called prophet (*1 John 4:1*). Paul again wrote concern for judging true prophecy: "*Don't stifle the Spirit. Don't despise prophecies, but test all things. Hold on to what is good (1 Thessalonians 5:19-21 NASB)."* All of these Scriptures place a unique responsibility on those with the Gift of Prophecy: to be certain that what is being spoken truly comes directly from God.

The Gift of Prophecy is a perceived revelation of what God is saying to the Church. The person with the Gift is responsible for interpreting the impression they are receiving in the Spirit. For this reason, I encourage any who may have the Gift of Prophecy to exercise additional caution in how they present a prophetic word: be humble, suppress pride which may have you say, "Thus says the Lord" when finished speaking. The judgement of whether it is directly from the Lord is the responsibility of other prophets in the church, not your own, as Paul writes in 1 Corinthians 14:29-33.

Those with the Gift of Prophecy are not God's ventriloquist dummies. They are New Covenant believers, filled with the Holy Spirit, whose personhood is not stripped from them, but rather used by God to convey His heart in a certain way. Prophecy may be directive, and it often is, or even predictive, as Scripture shows, but those with the Gift of Prophecy must be careful not to cross the line into the realm of soothsaying and divination as they may be tempted to for their own celebration and acknowledgement.

We do not have to accept all so-called prophecies, but the modern Church is often too quick to be suspicious of all prophecy. Rather than test it against the Word of God many people dismiss it entirely. I think this is an excellent reminder for today's Church: test the prophecy and whatever is found to be true hold on to it. Someone with the Gift of Prophecy is not God Himself, and as such it is conceivable that as an individual begins to receive Prophecy through the Gift of the Holy Spirit part of his self may become mixed with what is directly inspired by God. Jesus is the Prophet that Moses spoke of in Deuteronomy 18. He is the only person to ever hold the office of Prophet perfectly. As the Son of God, He carries the spirit of prophecy even from the beginning of the world. We, through salvation, redemption, and Baptism in the Holy Spirit, can receive in part His spirit of prophecy. This is why Paul said that we only prophesy in part. Therefore those giving a prophecy and those receiving it with their ears must be humble enough to consider its potential flaws and judge it by Scripture.

For this reason, I encourage you to consider that just as you may cut around the bone of a Porterhouse steak to enjoy the tender meat, so is true of prophecy that you may need to take that which is for your benefit and discard the parts that may bring spiritual harm. Prophecy can very often be a promise from God of things to come, but that does not mean that those words do not need to be shepherded by the Word. We must constantly submit ourselves to how and when God may want this promise to unfold. Moreover, we must take such words before the altar of God and be willing to sacrifice them to His unknown Will and timing. This is perhaps especially true if the words are not genuinely prophetic, but have enraptured our sensibilities.

God is concerned with the affect a prophecy may have on our lives. Shepherding a prophetic word takes care in seeking an interpretation from God of its meaning and timing, as well as its fulfillment. True prophecy will prove itself to be a revelation, a fresh perspective or an epiphany, of what Scripture already tells us in some way. Prophecy will illuminate the Word and make it the living and active Sword it truly is. Prophecy brings an understanding of God's plans and purposes outlined in Scripture off the pages and into our understanding in a way that we can grasp it.

As we begin to move in the Gift of Prophecy we must remember that we are being tasked with sharing God's divine purpose with whomever it is to be shared. Do not take this lightly, but do not be so fearful as to withhold the gift God is giving. From the moment we receive a prophetic word in the Spirit to the moment we speak it out, there seems to be a natural progression of processing that word.

First, we receive. In whatever way we receive it we must discern its origin—is it from the Holy Spirit? Next, we seek interpretation or understanding. Does it need interpreting or is it direct? If it requires more understanding we should ask God for clarity, especially if it comes during a time of private ministry. Third, we must ask God the means and manner in which to give the word. What degree of sensitivity and privacy is necessary? Some words are bold and strong, but God can direct us to give the word in a soft and gentle way. God will know how the person will best receive the word and so we must remain in the Spirit sensitive to the guidance of the Holy Spirit even after we have received a prophetic word.

All prophetic words are subject to judgement as Paul said. Just because Prophecy is a Gift that works in the supernatural power of the Holy Spirit does not mean that there is not any kind of order to its operation. Order in the church service is important. At the end of 1 Corinthians 14, Paul encouraged everyone to desire to prophesy and gave instructions that "*all things should be done with regard to decency and propriety and in an orderly fashion (1 Corinthians 14:40 AMP)*."

Prophecy should not contradict what the Holy Spirit is saying and doing during a gathering or church service. It should not interrupt the preacher from bringing the Word. While those moving in the Gift of Prophecy may sense an urgency to speak the word, Paul said, "*prophets' spirits are under the control of the prophets, since God is not a God of disorder but of peace (1 Corinthians 14:32-33a HCSB).*" Anyone operating in the Gift of Prophecy has the power to subject the spirit of prophecy to the order of the Holy Spirit.

When Paul suggested that two or three should be exercising the Gift and working together to judge what is spoken I believe it is out of a desire to ensure order. Like a litmus test, all prophecy, must achieve a certain level of basic edification, exhortation, or consolation. Prophecy will always magnify Christ—the Son of God, the Sacrificial Lamb, He who sits at the right hand of God the Father. Those with the Gift of Prophecy should focus on only speaking words that edify, exhort, and comfort. Even if this individual is receiving an impression of sickness, hardship, or tragedy they should exercise great caution in speaking it out, especially publicly. Instead I would encourage that person to first take it to the Lord in prayer for clearer understanding and confirmation before speaking it. Additionally, I believe wisdom would have the individual share it with someone else with the Gift of Prophecy to help discern before sharing it publicly. A prophetic word may reveal a coming hardship, but it will always bring with it hope and encouragement of God's faithfulness. God will not speak to His people harshly without reminding us of the hope we have through relationship with Him made available through Christ's death on the cross.

Prophecy should never be used to embarrass, shame, rebuke, discourage, or even publicly correct individual people. Prophecy will bring an endorsement of God's favor rather than condemnation and reassurance rather than discouragement. This does not mean that prophecy will not be used to bring conviction. In fact, to an unbeliever the prophetic is perhaps one of the greatest evangelistic tools other than a Word of Knowledge. The nature of prophecy as bringing encouragement shows that it will be used by God to defeat Satan's lies, his accusations, and any psychological attacks. Paul reminded Timothy of the prophecy spoken that released a mantle of ministry in Timothy's life and imparted a certain gift (*1 Timothy 4:14*).

These prophetic words grounded Timothy to "*fight the good fight, keeping faith and good conscience (1 Timothy 1:18 NASB).*" True prophetic words can often help us navigate our lives. They can bring us peace and calm in the middle of a waiting season. They can even bring us direction of either what to do or what not to do in a situation. However, prophetic words should not be treated as the definitive road map to reach God's will for your life. A single prophetic word should never be the only thing guiding you.

It is helpful to ask certain questions to test the validity of a prophecy, both as one giving a prophetic word and as one to whom a word is spoken. Judging a prophetic word is important as we continue to seek God's Will in our lives. We should be wholly led by the Holy Spirit and the Word of God when looking for life direction. We should never be solely reliant on a single prophetic word. We should ask:
- Has it been fulfilled?
- Is there conditional fulfillment (i.e. "if, then")?
- Is it Scriptural—either directly from Scripture or in alignment with the Truth?
- Has it been judged by the church as genuine?
- Is there confirmation in your spirit?
- Do you have true peace about this word?

- Does the word come in love even if it is rough?
- Does the messenger bear the Fruit of the Spirit?
- Does it convey a burden of the Lord?
- Does it uplift and speak to the Lordship of Jesus?
- Does it edify, exhort, or console God's people?

Prophecies can come from a variety of places and persons. We can receive prophesy through our own relationship with the Lord in a vision, a dream, an inner voice, an audible voice, an impression, etc. Often prophetic words come to us through those who operate frequently in the Gift of Prophecy and may even be called to the office of Prophet, like Elijah. Regardless of how this word comes it must be weighed and measured—tested and verified. Perhaps even most importantly prophecy should be constantly fostered with a humble attitude that its fulfillment may come with unexpected timing or in a totally unexpected way. However, you must step out in faith if you believe you are receiving a prophetic word. Paul said, "*Having gifts that differ according to the grace given to us, let us use them: if prophecy, in proportion to our faith (Romans 12:6 ESV).*"

You can only pour out on others something that you yourself possess. Consistently operating in the Gift of Prophecy is a process and we must be patient with His timing and His seasons, learning whatever it is to refine us as we present His message. If you have begun to move in the Gift of Prophecy, find another individual who is more mature in using that Gift from whom you can learn. Whatever your experience in being used by God to speak prophetically, you must be sensitive to only minister within the spiritual territory He has given you. Do not attempt to minister prophetically beyond your degree of maturity. The Lord will equip, anoint, and appoint you for specific times and places. If His Spirit has not commissioned you to move in public prophetic ministry, you may be open to spiritual attacks. Be sensitive to the Holy Spirit and humble to His leading. Be content where He has placed you and faithful to prove yourself able to move beyond the territory He has given you. Do not step out beyond what He has given you.

Remain humble. One of the greatest warnings is when pride begins to creep in. You must be humble enough to allow whatever prophetic words you speak to be judged and to accept any correction that may come with it. Paul was clear that those moving in the Gift of Prophecy are not like the solo Prophets of the Old Testament. If you begin to rely too heavily on your own self, you will be vulnerable to pride and deception to the point of being used as an instrument of the Enemy to draw people away from where the Spirit is leading.

As you begin to move in the Gift of Prophecy you should become increasingly compelled toward accuracy in the prophetic words you speak. Paul told the church in Corinth that we only prophesy in part (*1 Corinthians 13:9*). Increased accuracy will come with an increased intimacy with Christ. The more you know Him through His Word and through talking with Him, the more you will be able to discern if and when you are misinterpreting what the Spirit is saying. Jesus said that His sheep know His voice. The more intimate with Jesus you become, the more you will be able to separate His voice from any others trying to influence your presentation of what the Spirit is saying.

Discernings of Spirits
Personal Judgement or
Divine Perception?

"and to another discernings of spirits..."
1 Corinthians 12:10c YLT

God has appointed to each member of the body of Christ a Gift to edify and unify the Church, so that it may move in the power of the Holy Spirit unhindered by any other spirit that would seek to cause division. In other words, the Church of Jesus that ushers in His second coming will need all the Gifts in operation. This particular Gift of Revelation used within the church will help to identify areas in the church community that need to be addressed. The Discernings of Spirits is the ability to detect, recognize, distinguish, and identify the motivations of man and the spirits in operation behind those motivations. This Gift's importance will only increase as the second arrival of Christ approaches. The Bible repeatedly warns us that in the End Times deception will be the *modus operandi* of the Enemy. *"But the Spirit explicitly says that in later times some will fall away from the faith, paying attention to deceitful spirits and doctrines of demons... (1 Timothy 4:1 NASB)."*

Just as with Gifts of Healings, the Discernings of Spirits Gift shares the distinction of dual plurality. To clarify, the word "discernings" indicates that some people may be more sensitive to discerning specific spirits in accordance with their Gifts, ministries, and/or positions of leadership in the church. For example, a pastor may discern any of the various spirits as they affect the cohesive ministries of the church. Anyone involved in a ministry within the local church must understand that all Christian ministries occur in the spirit realm. Otherwise what a church may call ministry is effectively mere counsel, activity, or education. This Gift operates so that we can minister freedom, either to our own soul or to someone else. To minister to human needs without the discernment of evil spirits or forces is like a boxer who never lands a hit, but wears himself out swinging at the air (*1 Corinthians 9:26 NASB*).

For those to whom the Gift of Discernings of Spirits has been given, I want to place an emphasis on the importance of knowing, understanding, and believing Ephesians 6:12. Paul's letter to the Church in Ephesus was written as an encouragement to the believers there. He was intent on giving them instructions on how to hold on to the strong faith that sets them apart. He gave instructions for continued right living and right relationship among believers. Paul ended his letter to the Ephesians with the Armor of God and prefaced it with the reason for the armor in verse 12:

> *"For our struggle is not against flesh and blood, but against the rulers, against the powers, against the world forces of this darkness, against the spiritual forces of wickedness in the heavenly places."*
> *Ephesians 6:12 NASB*

The Gift of Discernings of Spirits is important for the church to acknowledge and recognize these rulers, powers, and forces that influence this world. A Word of Knowledge can often work in tandem with the Discerning of a spirit by giving Knowledge of a spirit, which helps to address and identify that it is wickedness at work and not the person alone.

Regardless of what translation you read, it is clear that 1 Corinthians 12:10c makes the distinction there are multiple spirits to be discerned. I think it is helpful to define what may be meant by "spirit" here. A spirit is a non-physical aspect of a being that has specific motivations unique to its being. As such, there are four spirits to be considered as discernible with respect to this Scripture verse: [1]the Spirit of God—Holy Spirit, [2]the spirit of Angels—good and evil, [3]Unclean Spirits—demons, and [4]the Spirit of Man—Self.

Discerning which of these spirits is directing and motivating the actions of humans is critical in Christian ministry. If an event is being led or directed by the Holy Spirit working through an individual, it should have the support and encouragement of church leadership. If an event is being led by an individual who is motivated by the desire for self glory, then church leadership would want to redirect that person's focus back to all things being done for the honor and glory of God alone. In ministering to someone incapable of disciplining themselves out of wrong actions, Discernings of Spirits will help to identify whether that individual needs deliverance of an unclean spirit or needs continued instruction in Scripture to experience freedom.

Discerning the Spirit of God is just as important as discerning any one of the other spirits. The Holy Spirit testifies to the character and nature of God the Father. His actions and the direction in which He leads people will always be consistent with the Word of God because all Scripture is given by God. The Spirit of God cannot contradict itself. The Holy Spirit will inspire individuals to obey Scripture, encourage one another, comfort one another, and guide people into Truth out of genuine love and concern for them. The Spirit of God will never incite division among believers.

The Holy Spirit was given to the Believers in Christ as a Helper and Comforter. The Gifts that flow out of the Baptism of the Holy Spirit are to create unity among the members of the body of Christ and to minister to a lost and dying world. The Spirit of God will never function as self-seeking; it will always point back to the Father. The Holy Spirit will provoke us to intercede for people (*Romans 8:27*). Discerning the Spirit of God is important for allowing individuals to step out in the Gifts of the Spirit in a church. If it is not the Holy Spirit inspiring a prophetic word or a word of knowledge, it could be destructive to the well being of that local church or divisive in that congregation. Church leaders should eagerly desire this Gift so that they can continue to lead their members into a deeper relationship with Jesus and revelation of His nature.

The spirit of Angels, both good and evil, must be discerned to know who is the messenger and from where is the message coming. Angels are consistently referred to as messengers in the Old Testament. It is important to remember that Satan himself was an angel—a cherub named Lucifer—and when he fell from heaven he took angels with him (*Isaiah 14:12-15 NKJV*, *Ezekiel 28:12-19 NASB*, *Revelation 12:9 NASB*). Discerning the spirit of Angels will also mean discerning their allegiance and whether it is to God or to Satan.

Discerning the origin of the message will help determine the allegiance of the angel. Angels appear with the Lord when He visits Abraham to tell him of the promised son, Isaac (*Genesis 18:1-15*). Two angels then visit Lot in Sodom to warn him of the impending judgement and destruction coming (*Genesis 19:1-13*). So, we see that God's angels come to bring good news and warnings of judgement. Of course, there are many more examples of God's messengers coming to bring messages to His people. Paul warned that Satan himself will even appear as an angel of light (*2 Corinthians 11:14*). Jesus explained in Matthew 25:41 that when the day of judgement comes there has been a place of eternal fire prepared for Satan and his angels. Paul warned in Colossians 2:18 that evil angels will pursue being worshipped themselves. This is consistent with

Isaiah 14:13 where we derive the understanding that the angel Lucifer initially desired to be worshipped and this led to his fall from grace.

Unclean spirits or demons are often the most commonly thought of spirits when referring to the Discernings of Spirits Gift. While discerning these spirits is critical to the life and health of a church and for Christian counseling and ministry, it is not any more important than discerning the other kinds of spirits. In fact, I would warn anyone of being overly concerned or curious about demons and their workings to deceive man. Sometimes a concentrated study on one particular subject distracts us from focusing on the more important topic. The glory of God overcomes the control unclean spirits can have and as such our study of His salvation and power over Satan and his forces should be the larger focus. That being said, the discerning of these spirits in all their variety is helpful in ministering deliverance and in seeing the Lord work to set people free of evil forces that control them.

One great example of a person being influenced by an unclean spirit comes from Job 4:15-21. Here Job's friend, Eliphaz, was visited by a spirit who brought a line of questioning that condemned Job's character. What this spirit provoked in Eliphaz was the belief that Job was not favored by God or found blameless at all, but rather Job was guilty and God was punishing him. We know this to be the influence of an unclean spirit because it is entirely contradictory to Job 1:8. Although this spirit is not given a name as are those given in the following examples, it would seem very clear that this spirit is unclean as it is peddling confusion and deception about Job's character.

The Gospel writer Luke seems to have been particularly fond of details. This is not surprising given his occupation as a physician (*Colossians 4:14*). He recorded Jesus' ministry with great detail especially with respect to Healings. Luke is also responsible for the next three examples where unclean spirits were identified through Discernings of Spirits. Luke recorded Jesus healing on the Sabbath in Luke 13:10-17. As He was in a synagogue, a woman who was sick and could not stand up straight was there. Luke identified her malady as such: *"and lo, there was a woman having a spirit of infirmity eighteen years, and she was bowed together, and not able to bend back at all... (Luke 13:11 YLT)."* She received physical healing, but only after Jesus commanded that she be released from that spirit of infirmity (*Luke 13:12*).

Luke is also attributed with penning the Book of the Acts of the Apostles. Since Luke was a known traveling companion of the Apostle Paul the last two examples of Discernings of Spirits comes from Paul's ministry. The first example is from Paul traveling out on a missionary journey to Cyprus. There he encountered a magician and false prophet, Elymas, who began to speak against Paul. Luke wrote that Paul was filled with the Holy Spirit, stared straight at Elymas, rebuked the spirit in him, and said, *"You who are full of all deceit and fraud, you son of the devil, you enemy of all righteousness... (Acts 13:10 NASB)."*

The second example is a slave girl who practiced fortune telling in Thyatira (*Acts 16:16-22*). Luke identified her as actually having an unclean spirit that gave her this power and not a prophetic gift: *"a slave-girl having a spirit of divination met us... (Acts 16:16a NASB)."* It is important to note that everything she spoke was the truth. Still, Paul was annoyed by her proclamations because he knew they were not coming from the witness of the Holy Spirit. For this reason, Paul commanded the spirit to come out of her (*Acts 16:18*).

Lastly, and perhaps sometimes the most difficult for us, is discerning whether an action or its motivation comes from the Spirit of Man—Self. The Spirit of Man is made known through our character; it is the nature of man. King David, the prophet Jeremiah, the Apostle Paul, and Jesus Himself lamented the deceitfulness of man's heart and his unrighteousness. The Spirit of Man is selfish, it resists and rebels against God. As Jesus sat with His disciples to tell them of His impending suffering and death, Peter famously said in Matthew 16:22 and Mark 8:32 that he did not believe it would happen. Jesus identified Peter's motivation and rebuked his selfish comment: *"Get behind Me, Satan! You are a stumbling block to Me; for you are not setting your mind on God's interests, but man's (Matthew 16:23 NASB)."* The word "Satan" here is translated from the Greek word for adversary or opposer. In fact, Jesus was identifying Peter's comment as opposing the will of God. Jesus knew this was not the Holy Spirit, an angel, or an unclean spirit. His rebuke was discerning the nature of man—Self—in Peter.

In Acts, Luke described Stephen's encounter with the Council and their accusation of blaspheme against him. Stephen discerned what spirit was at work in these men—the Spirit of Man—that would be so rebellious against the move of God: *"You men who are stiff-necked and uncircumcised in heart and ears are always resisting the Holy Spirit; you are doing just as your fathers did (Acts 7:51 NASB)."*

The Purposes of this Gift are not to judge other people in their actions or motivations for self-righteous or self-promoting reasons. When the Holy Spirit gives this Gift to people in Christ's church it is to be used by God to set people free. There are four clear purposes of this Gift. The first is that it lifts the veil separating us from the spiritual world. Paul explained that just as a veil separated the Israelites from the glory of God, there is a veil in the spirit realm that can be lifted through the power of the Holy Spirit.

> *"14But their minds were hardened; for until this very day at the reading of the old covenant the same veil remains unlifted, because it is removed in Christ. 15But to this day whenever Moses is read, a veil lies over their heart; 16but whenever a person turns to the Lord, the veil is taken away."*
> *2 Corinthians 3:14-16 NASB*

We know from Daniel 10 and Ephesians 6 that there is an unseen battle in the air against God's forces and Satan's forces. The veil in the temple was torn when Christ committed His spirit to God the Father (*Matthew 27:50-51*). The significance of that is not lost on Paul when he wrote to the Church in Corinth in 2 Corinthians 3. The veil has already been torn to give us access to seeing into the spirit and through the Holy Spirit we can discern what forces are at work in motivating the actions of people.

The second purpose is to give us God's eyes to see things as He sees them. As Samuel sought out the next anointed king of Israel, God taught him that He looks into a man's heart and discerns his intentions.

> *"But the Lord said to Samuel, "Do not look at his appearance or at the height of his stature, because I have rejected him; for God sees not as man sees, for man looks at the outward appearance, but the Lord looks at the heart." 1 Samuel 16:7 NASB*

Paul wrote in Hebrews 4:12 that God Himself discerns the thoughts of a man and is able to separate spirit from soul (i.e. the Self). This Gift of the Spirit allows us to see as God sees and to discern what is from another spirit or from Self. King David recognized this, as well, when we wrote that a man sees himself as righteous, but *"Jehovah is pondering the spirits (Proverbs 16:2b YLT)."* When we see as God sees, we step away from our inclination to judge people's actions or motivations from a self-righteous perspective. I firmly believe as this Gift operates in us, we can discern so clearly that we are compelled to compassion when we discern any spirit other than the Holy Spirit leading or controlling a person. Christ is our example when He had compassion on the demon possessed boy who threw himself in fire and water (*Matthew 17:15* and *Mark 9:22*).

The third purpose has already been mentioned briefly: to protect us from deception. As we now understand from the four different kinds of spirits that have an influence in this world, there is a need to discern what is directing the actions of individuals. John confirmed that not every spirit is from the Lord and they must be discerned because there are false prophets (*1 John 4:1*). John wrote in the Book of Revelation what he saw in the spirit in the End Times:

> *"¹³And I saw coming out of the mouth of the dragon and out of the mouth of the beast and out of the mouth of the false prophet, three unclean spirits like frogs; ¹⁴for they are spirits of demons, performing signs, which go out to the kings of the whole world, to gather them together for the war of the great day of God, the Almighty." Revelation 16:13-14 NASB*

The deception that has been prophesied should compel us to desire this Gift so that we may not ourselves be deceived and to help guide the Church into seeing the spirits that have come to deceive God's people. Jesus warned that some will be led by spirits, other than the Spirit of God, who are deceived themselves and used to deceive others (*Matthew 24:24*). We must be vigilant and understand that this Gift's operation in the Church is critical to the health of a congregation, so that no division and deception can flourish.

The fourth purpose is that this Gift enables us to diagnose people's problems and to help them. It equips the Church for Christian ministry to a person by giving vision into the spirit realm to discern the root of the issue. One example of this has already been given from Luke 13:11-12. The woman needed deliverance from a spirit of infirmity in order to receive healing in her back. Jesus said, "*Woman, thou hast been loosed from thy infirmity (Luke 13:12 YLT)*." It is after her deliverance that she was healed. Again, discerning an unclean spirit and ministering deliverance will address the root of the problem, such as an illness. In our modern world we would probably diagnose the boy who was mute, convulsing, and foaming at the mouth with epilepsy. His father, the disciples, and Jesus understood it was an unclean spirit. As soon as he was delivered of that spirit he was cured (*Matthew 17:18*).

This fourth purpose is most explicitly seen in the deliverance of people from unclean spirits. Take one more example: the Gadarene demoniac in Mark 5:1-20 is clearly thought to be psychotic. Once he received deliverance he became sane and testified of his deliverance. While I think these examples give the clearest insight into this purpose, discerning whether our thoughts and actions are under the direction of the Spirit of God or the Spirit of Man will help us to receive freedom. As we can discern our own Self-thoughts by the help of the Holy Spirit we can begin to discipline ourselves into right thinking.

When we understand that the battle we face is in the spirit realm, we can know that just as there is an order in war between nations there is an order in spiritual warfare. This Gift of Discernings of Spirits helps to identify the nature of the thing we are battling. We must know who or what is the enemy or from where our motivations are coming, otherwise it is like going to war with the wrong country. Once the kind of spirit has been identified through this Gift, then we are responsible to reject the influence of any spirit other than the Holy Spirit. By an act of our will we can reject these spirits, turn away from Satan, and turn to the Lord who has so much promised for us. James wrote instructions for this:

> *"⁷Submit therefore to God. Resist the devil and he will flee from you. ⁸Draw near to God and He will draw near to you. Cleanse your hands, you sinners; and purify your hearts, you double-minded... ¹⁰Humble yourselves in the presence of the Lord, and He will exalt you." James 4:7-8, 10 NASB*

This Gift truly helps to set people free from evil influence and ransom them back into the Kingdom of God to receive their destiny. Rejecting these spirits is only part of receiving that freedom. You can reject a thing, but turning away from it and denying it as a temptation is a separate act of the will. When Jesus appeared to Saul on the road to Damascus and appointed him to minister the Gospel He described the purpose of Saul's mission as such:

> *"to open their eyes so that they may turn from darkness to light and from the dominion of Satan to God, that they may receive forgiveness of sins and an inheritance..." Acts 26:18 NASB*

The verses from James and Acts help to explain the four stages of spiritual warfare: recognize, reject, rebuke, and repent.

Even while we grow in this Gift, we must continue to have reverence for Biblical discernment that comes from Scripture directly. It is important to understand that this Gift works in harmony with Biblical discernment. In fact, Biblical discernment aids supernatural discernment by giving your soul a defense for your discernment. In other words, Biblical discernment, which comes directly from Scripture, helps to keep us from straying into an attitude of spiritual elitism and self-righteous judgement.

John wrote about testing or determining the spirit that is at work in people. He provided us with one definitive test to determine if a spirit is not from God:

> *"2By this you know the Spirit of God: every spirit that confesses that Jesus Christ has come in the flesh is from God; 3and every spirit that does not confess Jesus is not from God; this is the spirit of the antichrist, of which you have heard that it is coming, and now it is already in the world."*
>
> *1 John 4:2-3 NASB*

We know that we can use Scripture to discern because in the verse proceeding these, John wrote, "*Beloved, do not believe every spirit, but test the spirits to see whether they are from God, because many false prophets have gone out into the world (1 John 4:1 NASB).*" We can test spirits and we can use Scripture as a weapon of spiritual discernment and warfare.

Like the other Gifts of Revelation, as you begin to experience this Gift in operation through you, it is important to test your discernment using the Word of God and to take that discernment before the Lord. Discernings of Spirits is for Christian ministry such as deliverance and counseling. It is important to intercede for the person receiving ministry to be open to receive what the Holy Spirit is revealing and speaking through the Gifts of Revelation.

Tongues and Interpretation of Tongues
Random Babbling or God Speaking?

"to another various kinds of tongues, and to another the interpretation of tongues."
1 Corinthians 12:10d NASB

The first Gift of the Holy Spirit that began functioning through the 120 disciples gathered in the Upper Room at Pentecost was the Gift of Tongues. No matter which translation you read of Acts Chapter 2, you will discover that tongues appeared like fire, rested on the disciples, and baptized them in the Holy Spirit. Then they *"began to speak in different languages, as the Spirit gave them ability for speech (Acts 2:4 HCSB)."* As we read further in Acts 2 Luke described these Galilean disciples as preaching the Gospel in the many native languages of Jews present in Jerusalem at that time. The Gift of Tongues is really a supernatural gift of a language unknown to the speaker. While hearing Tongues spoken in Church for the first time can be a bit unsettling (if we're honest) we must understand that it is ordained in Scripture by God and its purpose is for the building up of His Church in several ways. The phrase "various kinds of tongues" indicates that the act of speaking in Tongues has multiple uses or purposes.

The Gift of Tongues is the power to speak what the Spirit is saying in a language other than one(s) you have learned naturally. In the case of Acts 2, the Gift was used to preach the Gospel to those who had not heard it yet. The Gift of Tongues can be used as a witness or a sign to unbelievers. When Paul explained the Gifts of the Spirit to the Church in Corinth he did it this way:

> *"²¹It is written in the law: I will speak to these people of other languages and by the lips of foreigners, and even then, they will not listen to Me, says the Lord. ²²It follows that speaking in other languages is intended as a sign, not for believers but for unbelievers." 1 Corinthians 14:21-22a* HCSB

On the day of Pentecost, the Jews in Jerusalem that heard the Gospel in their native languages were enraptured by the reality that Jews from Galilee would have command of such vast and varied languages as to preach to Jews from across the known world. In other words, it is because the disciples were speaking in languages they could not possibly know that these Jews were interested and attentive to *what* the disciples were saying.

It is clear from evidence in Scripture that the spontaneous speaking in unknown words follows the Baptism of the Holy Spirit. The disciples in the Upper Room (*Acts 2:1-4*), Cornelius' family and friends (*Acts 10:44-46*), and believers in Ephesus (*Acts 19:1-6*) all experienced this phenomenon. Some even believe that the sign Simon observed of the Baptism of the Holy Spirit in Samaria was the spontaneous speaking in Tongues because it is the only consistently attributed evidence that an individual has received the Baptism. It is this outward, audible sign of the Baptism that knitted together the early Church. They knew one another as Christians by this sign. The speaking in Tongues is an evidence to other believers that you have truly been Baptized in the Holy Spirit. If you had not been Baptized, you would not speak in Tongues. Before Christ ascended to Heaven after His resurrection He attributed the speaking of Tongues as a sign of believers: "*And these signs will accompany those who believe...they will speak in new tongues (Mark 16:17 ESV)*."

When someone first receives the Baptism of the Holy Spirit they may begin to spontaneously utter sounds, syllables, and even words that their natural mind does not understand. This is more commonly considered the receiving of a "prayer language," which would be a specific kind or use of the Gift of Tongues. If you believe that you have received the Baptism, but have not spoken in an unknown language, yield your mind and your tongue to the Spirit. In our prayer language we can choose to articulate sounds by the opening of our mouths and the moving of our lips, but it is the Spirit that forms the syllables through our tongues. I believe that a prayer language often manifests as the first experience or use of the Gift of Tongues for a new Spirit-filled believer. If you do not learn to pray in the Spirit with your prayer language in private, how can you be expected to yield your tongue enough to speak publicly to the congregation in a Tongue?!

James reminded us of the wicked nature of the tongue and its need to be tamed (*James 3:5-10*). While the tongue cannot be tamed by man this is proof to me that it is only by the work of the Holy Spirit that it could ever be tamed to speak in an unknown language. While the tongue is a problem for many people, its true purpose is to praise and bring glory to God. The Gift of Tongues is the work of the Holy Spirit to bring into submission this problem faculty of humanity. Therefore, prayer language as the first typification of the Gift of Tongues is a way for us to learn how to yield and discipline our tongues to be used only for the glory of God. Perhaps James' observation is also why so many Christian believers, even those who profess belief that the Gifts of the Holy Spirit are for the present-day Church, struggle with the notion of speaking in Tongues.

A prayer language, available only with the Baptism of the Holy Spirit, unlocks a new relationship with the Lord. When Paul explained praying and speaking in Tongues in 1 Corinthians 14 he said, "*For if I pray in a tongue, my spirit prays but my mind is unfruitful (1 Corinthians 14:14 ESV).*" Privately praying in Tongues is between you and God; it works to edify your spirit (*1 Corinthians 14:4a*). This private prayer language is a work of the Spirit in you. The Spirit in you knows the direction in which to pray, while the natural mind may pray in a direction not wholly led by the Spirit. When you pray in the Spirit with Tongues, your spirit is strengthened over your natural man's spirit and its limited understanding of how to pray.

I believe praying in Tongues builds up your spirit thereby making your spirit more sensitive to the things and the direction of the Holy Spirit. The Baptism does not come without this new weapon of spiritual warfare. The Bible says, "*Pray at all times in the Spirit with every prayer and request... (Ephesians 6:18a HCSB)*" and "*Likewise the Spirit helps us in our weakness. For we do not know what to pray for as we ought, but the Spirit himself intercedes for us with groaning too deep for words (Romans 8:26 ESV).*" How could we possibly pray in the Spirit at all times without the ability to pray through the power of the Spirit with an unlimited vocabulary by which to intercede?

Praying in Tongues is the same initiation of the Baptism of the Holy Spirit received by believers recorded throughout the Book of Acts. It is the speaking in Tongues that introduces our spirit to the leading of the Holy Spirit. By yielding the use of our tongue we enter into a spiritual place where we are open to be used in any of the nine Spiritual Gifts. The Gift of Tongues is a work of the Spirit through you and is for the edification of the Church when an interpretation is given. Paul clarified this when he said that the manifestation of the Gifts in the assembly should be for the edification of the church. Paul called for an order to the manifestation of Tongues during church services. He explained that Tongues without an Interpretation are only for a communication between man and God, except for as a sign to unbelievers like in Acts 2:5-12.

The Gift of the Interpretation of Tongues is very clearly a separate Gift of the Holy Spirit. However, without Tongues this Gift has no purpose; it would be both meaningless and useless without the presence of an unknown language. The Gift of Interpretation is defined by its use. Interpretation here is the supernaturally imparted ability to deliver the same word as that given in a Tongue in a known language of the hearers. It is quite literally interpreting an unknown language into a known language, but only through the power of the Holy Spirit and not through the use of the human intellect. Having a natural disposition to pick up and learn languages quickly does not mean that you have either Spiritual Gifts of Tongues or Interpretation. This is entirely a Holy Spirit directed ability. Paul encouraged whoever spoke in a Tongue to also pray for the Interpretation, so while these Gifts may be present in two unique individuals it is also possible that one individual may possess both Spiritual Gifts.

If then, Tongues are given aloud during the assembly of believers, Paul said there should not be more than two or three spoken and someone must give an Interpretation. Otherwise the speaking of Tongues does not benefit the rest of the congregation in "*revelation or knowledge or prophecy or teaching (1 Corinthians 14:6 ESV).*" Therefore, if a Tongue is given aloud, then an Interpretation must be given for the building up of the church. "*But if there is no interpreter, that person should keep silent in the church and speak to himself and to God (1 Corinthians 14:28 HCSB).*"

It's interesting that Paul should mention the presence of an Interpreter here. In 1 Corinthians 12, Paul established that God placed these Gifts in the Church and those to move in these Gifts. An Interpreter is one with the Gift of the Interpretation of Tongues. If a Tongue is given in the assembly, through the Gift of Tongues, then it is necessary that an Interpretation of that Tongue be given in order to build up the church. Paul encouraged the Church in Corinth that because they were so eager to see the Gifts of the Spirit present among them during their assemblies that they should strive to edify the Church.

Since the edification of the church body can only take place either through Prophecy or the Interpretation of Tongues (*1 Corinthians 14:3-5*), then we can understand that when a Tongue and its Interpretation are given in an assembly it is the same as if a Prophecy was spoken. Paul said that Prophecy was greater than Tongues, unless an Interpretation was given. God would not speak to His Church only to not be understood. If He speaks through someone with the Gift of Tongues, then He will provide its understanding through an Interpretation.

> "*In the same way, unless you use your tongue for intelligible speech, how will what is spoken be known? For you will be speaking into the air... Therefore the person who speaks in another language should pray that he can interpret.*"
> *1 Corinthians 14:9 & 13 HCSB*

The use and presence of Tongues in an assembly should not leave the congregation confused or disillusioned with the Spirit of God. In order for the Tongue and its Interpretation to be for the assembly and not just for the private edification of the individuals, the Tongue and its Interpretation must be judged.

Just as the test for Prophecy is whether the word edifies, exhorts, or comforts, so is the test for the joint giving of a Tongue and its Interpretation in the assembly. Paul's call for an Interpretation to follow after every Tongue and limiting the number of Tongues given to just three indicates the need for order in the assembly so that people receive what the Spirit of God is saying in both their spirits and their minds. We cannot be encouraged in our minds nor our minds be renewed if only our spirit is being ministered to and built up. Ultimately, edification and order must be present in the assembly when either a Prophecy or a Tongue and its Interpretation are given. Paul is clear, *"All things must be done for edification (1 Corinthians 14:26b HCSB)."*

When Paul said that Prophecy is greater than speaking with Tongues it is only due to the impact that these two Gifts have on the congregation as a whole. However, if an individual receives both Tongues and its Interpretation, then he is able to minister through the Spirit of God similar to Prophecy (*1 Corinthians 14:5*). Prophecy affords a direct and clear word from God. Tongues require waiting on the Interpretation before the word can be understood. I believe this is why Paul proclaimed Prophecy to be a greater Gift. The phrase "lost in translation" can be applied to this distinction. Just as Prophecy may come filtered through an individual, with Tongues and an Interpretation that leaves more room for filtered expressions of the Spirit.

Additionally, a member of the congregation may only receive part of the Interpretation and another member may not be faithful to give the remainder of the Interpretation of a Tongue. Hence Paul's encouragement, *"Pursue love and desire the spiritual gifts, and above all that you may prophesy (1 Corinthians 14:1 HCSB)."*

The following question arises: If Prophecy is a greater Gift, then why would God give us two "lesser" Gifts that would have to be used together to achieve the same end? Why have Prophecy *and* Tongues and Interpretation? I believe Paul answered this question in 1 Corinthians 12 when he first listed the nine Spiritual Gifts. We need *all* the Gifts working together in the Church for the building up of the Church and for ministering the glory of God. We are equipped with the Spiritual Gifts because Christ left us with the Holy Spirit to enable us to minister the Gospel in the same way Christ did when He walked the earth—tangibly. God wants His Church to be one body. He calls us to be wholly dependent on Him and interdependent on our brothers and sisters in Christ. Paul described the Church as a body with many parts that cannot say to one another they have no need of each other. *"If all were a single member, where would the body be? As it is, there are many parts, yet one body (1 Corinthians 12:19-20 ESV)."* God in His divine wisdom knew our fallen, proud nature would disregard one another if we were not in need of one another to grow in Christian perfection.

I believe the need for Prophecy plus Tongues and Interpretation goes beyond just the unifying of the body of Christ. The Gift of Tongues is not just the submission of our mouths, but also our minds, to what the Spirit has to say. Therefore, the need for Tongues and Interpretation in addition to Prophecy is the humbling of humanity. These Gifts require that we set aside our natural thinking, acquired knowledge, and preconceived notions of how God would speak to His Church. In other words, it takes us off the throne and out of the spotlight and points back to God, giving Him all the glory. As we step out of the way it gives the Spirit freedom to reign.

This is so important for the Church to remember: It is never about the person through whom the Gift is being used. It must always be about God and His sovereign direction for His Church. The Holy Spirit was left for us in order to prepare Christ's Church to be His bride. The humbling of His Church through the work of His Holy Spirit is in order that the Church would be prepared as a bride holy and blameless (*Ephesians 5:23-27*). The essence of all nine Gifts is to prepare His Bride to be wholly dependent on Him for all our needs.

Lastly, I believe that there is a third reason for these Gifts to be simultaneously present in the Church. Ultimately, this reason and the last two reveal how we must constantly submit our spirit to the Spirit of God. If all should seek to Prophesy, then certainly all should seek to Interpret for the same goal of building up the Church. Tongues and its Interpretation binds a congregation together as the Tongue gets the attention and the call for an Interpretation should keep all in a posture of prayer asking for the Spirit to give the Interpretation. Since Tongues are unintelligible to the speaker and most often the hearers (the exception being cases like in Acts 2), it grabs the attention of people. Anyone hearing Tongues spoken in a service for the first time can identify that an unknown language was spoken much more easily than they may be able to identify a Prophecy. The character and nature of Tongues is that it grabs the attention of those listening and provokes them to consider what the

Spirit of God is speaking. If anyone is interested to know what the Tongue means, they begin to listen for the Interpretation. This is a third aspect of the humbling of humanity to hear and be led by the Holy Spirit.

If Prophecy could be considered the most mystical of the Gifts, then Tongues is certainly the most stereotypically weird Gift. This is usually the movement of the Holy Spirit that the modern American Christian immediately rejects as too bizarre to be from God. I've even heard some reject this Gift as being from the devil. It most certainly is not from the devil. As Christ so famously pointed out:

> "*Every kingdom divided against itself is headed for destruction, and a house divided against itself falls. If Satan also is divided against himself, how will his kingdom stand?" Luke 11:17-18a* HCSB

Praying in Tongues is praying by the power of the Spirit and it is the last piece of the Armor of God—the thrusting javelin that reaches its target with precision from afar. How could praying in Tongues be from the devil if it is so effective in overcoming his schemes?

Paul told the Corinthian church that he thanked God he prayed in Tongues more than all of them and then he said this:

> "*Therefore, my brothers, be eager to prophesy, and do not forbid speaking in other languages. But everything must be done decently and in order."*
> *1 Corinthians 14:39-40* HCSB

In the assembly of Christians, if a Tongue is given, wait on the Interpretation, ask the Spirit to bring Interpretation that the congregation may have an understanding of what the Spirit of God is saying and wants to do in the hearts and minds of His people.

Stepping out to be used by the Spirit in a Tongue can be an uneasy task, but be encouraged. The Spirit may be entrusting you with just one short phrase, yield so that your brothers and sisters in Christ may be encouraged. This goes for you, as well, when you begin to move in Interpretation. You may only receive a single word, but know that it is for the building up of the body of Christ.

Training Children in the Gifts of the Holy Spirit

"Train up a child in the way he should go, Even when he is old he will not depart from it." Proverbs 22:6 NASB

How we train our children determines their path in life. This is good or bad, positive or negative. Some often teach this verse in the Proverbs to be about moral or spiritual training and it is, but it does not indicate that the training is in the right direction. The Young's Literal Translation puts Proverbs 22:6 this way: *"Give instruction to a youth about his way, Even when he is old he turneth not from it."* This verse applies to everything we teach our kids. We teach them manners, hygiene, morals, and discipline. They learn our habits and the consequences, both good and bad, to every action. Children learn our pessimism. They are already optimistic. Little kids are funny. They will ask you for anything. If you tell them "no," it doesn't seem to affect their resolve to ask you again 5 minutes later or the next time they see you. Moreover they seem to ask with total confidence that you will give it to them.

Kids are eager to receive revelation of Jesus just as much as adults and they are not weighted down with the same skepticism and pessimism of "grown-ups." Kids have to be encouraged in their faith. I would venture to say that most kids already have an extraordinary amount of faith, but it needs to be channeled. Acts of Faith are committed best with the confident heart of a child. A good case can be made that this is what Jesus meant in Matthew 18. We can come to God the Father with requests like a child. Other Scriptures tell us that no father would give serpents and stones to children who ask for eggs and bread. So, we can go with confidence that God will give us what we ask.

While I do not believe that we must wait for the Baptism of the Holy Spirit, I do believe because of personal experience that we do not always immediately receive anything and everything we ask from or of God. If your kid asks for a cookie before dinner, they might have to wait. I would definitely not hand out sweet delicious dessert before broccoli, because then the broccoli will only taste worse. It's not that they can't have a cookie, but they need to eat a healthy dinner first. In other words, sometimes God makes us wait for what we ask until after we have taken in something He has planned for our good first. And you never know, maybe after dinner you want ice cream instead. If you had the cookie before dinner and then decided you wanted ice cream after, that usually doesn't fly with mom and dad. Of course this little metaphor doesn't cover all of the nuances of God's gifts to His children, but it helps illustrate for us that sometimes we're not always in tune with God's timing.

Let's extend this metaphor to include another scenario. What if mom had ice cream sundaes planned for after dinner? The child begs for a cookie and she gives it to him, but not without promising that there is better dessert after dinner. He takes the cookie and is crushed sitting at the table after dinner watching everyone else eat ice cream sundaes. Sometimes we're not in line with asking for God's Will. God's timing and God's Will are tricky things to know. Scripture helps us to understand some of this some of the time. Otherwise we need to have a submissive heart to when God says, "no" or "wait," and then we can come asking again not crushed or angry with God for denying us what we wanted when we wanted it.

Children are open to receive the Baptism of the Holy Spirit and all of the Gifts of the Holy Spirit. We must have the Baptism of the Holy Spirit to receive any of the Gifts of the Holy Spirit. We are responsible for teaching them that they are gifts to be received and can never be earned and that there is no age requirement for receiving these Gifts. Kids love to experience the presence of the Holy Spirit. It is tangible. They love the Gifts for the same reason: they make God real. His manifest power through the Gifts is observable—we experience them with one or more of our five natural senses. We should be encouraging children to ask for the Baptism of the Holy Spirit and continually be asking God for His Gifts. Once a child has received the Baptism of the Holy Spirit and at least one of the nine Gifts, he or she must be encouraged, taught, and trained in it. One of the greatest things to remember is that children receive all of Him when they receive the Baptism of the Holy Spirit. That means they can move in all of the nine Gifts just as powerfully and clearly as any adult. Paul encouraged Timothy in this when he mentioned Timothy's youth and his example to other believers (*1 Timothy 4:12*).

Just like any gift, they must be used otherwise what is the point?! How do children use gifts on birthdays and Christmases? They play with them. They practice how to be doctors or teachers. They might need training wheels on that new bike before they are ready to ride it on their own. If we want to see the Church grow in the movement of the Holy Spirit, we have to allow for times of training and practice, especially in our children, but for our adults, as well. That is what the church I grew up in allowed. It is so important that children understand the purpose of the Gifts. Our church's youth group recently experienced a powerful outpouring of the Holy Spirit. Many were Baptized and spontaneously began speaking in Tongues. They began laying hands on one another and our leaders praying in the Spirit. They were so filled with joy at the experience that they wanted to continue to experience His overwhelming presence. We allowed them to play and it was an unforgettable weekend.

Paul said that the Gifts of the Holy Spirit are available to all Christians with no special reservations for any particular age group, doctrinal group, or privileged few.

> "⁴Now there are varieties of gifts, but the same Spirit. ⁵And there are varieties of ministries, and the same Lord. ⁶There are varieties of effects, but the same God who works all things in all persons. ⁷But to each one is given the manifestation of the Spirit for the common good... ¹¹But one and the same Spirit works all these things, distributing to each one individually just as He wills." 1 Corinthians 12:4-7, 11 NASB

God gives these Gifts to all His children. He is not playing favorites. The Gifts are not "powers" like what superheroes have in comic books, they are supernatural and a manifestation of the Holy Spirit Himself. So, the Gifts are clearly for children and accessible to children. Children need to know the purpose of the Gifts so that their desire for them is purely in alignment with God's use and intention. These Gifts display God's power and authority over this natural world, and because of this they give us access to the heavenly realm where supernatural things occur. These Gifts confirm the Lordship of Jesus and establish the Church as His body by being used by the Spirit to convey God's desire to be in relationship with us.

Let's start with the Gift of Faith. This is the first Gift of the Holy Spirit I received as a child. I was probably 8 years old at the time. Sometimes the Gift of Faith shows itself as believing for something supernaturally extraordinary. Not everyone who has faith in God or is even Baptized in the Holy Spirit has the Gift of Faith. Even if you as an adult do not share such Faith with a child, do not discourage it. Teach them to pray for what they have Faith to see happen. Build them up to continue believing. Be excited with them to believe for whatever it is. Let them encourage you in your faith. In his letter to the church in Ephesus Paul wrote:

> *"Now to him who is able to do far more abundantly than all that we ask or think, according to the power at work within us, to him be glory in the church and in Christ Jesus throughout all generations, forever and ever. Amen." Ephesians 3:20 ESV*

Paul must have had the Gift of Faith because he understood that God still worked in extraordinarily supernatural ways. Paul knew that God was limitless in His power and that our own human understanding is what limits our access to His incredible creative and restorative power.

Childhood is excellent training ground for moving in Gifts of Healings and Effecting of Miracles. It is a perfect time to teach them to ask for and receive Healing and Miracles. Why? Children have not been discouraged by the reality that not everyone receives a Healing or deceived by theologies that distort what Scripture says about Healing. They do not try to provide a rationale for why we don't see a Healing. Children approach Jesus as fully capable and willing. All you have to tell kids is what Scripture says and share the numerous stories of Healing in the Bible. That's all they need and they accept God's truth without entertaining thoughts like "Did God really say...?" They need to be introduced to the reality of God's healing power, nature, and character. How do I know this to be true? I was one of them and I practice it with kids all the time. I give them simple truths in Scripture and ask them to apply it first. If we don't get the desired outcome, then we discuss it. Let me be clear, we don't always get a Healing or a Miracle. However, there is a difference between being open to the unbidden timing of the Will of God and having unbelief that He can or will.

I grew up in a church where Healings and Miracles took place a lot. Being around people who had Faith to see people healed was important in forming my own faith. My parents and a few others were great encouragers of our youth group to step out and pray for people to be healed, sometimes people we didn't even know. They gave us opportunity to practice our faith. They provided us with support and encouraged us to boldly ask God for Healings and Miracles. I was trained when to pray and how to pray. We saw God's glory manifested in our little country Methodist church.

We were encouraged constantly to pray for Healing for one another for all kinds of things like headaches, cuts and scrapes that come from being a kid. We were given opportunity to lay hands on one another and on adults to pray for Healing. We talked about it like it was normal. It was normal. It should be normal. How do you a train a child or even yourself to believe for Healing? You make it normal. You make it part of the expectation. How do you make it part of your expectations? Through faith. Romans 10:17 lays this out for us: faith comes from hearing the Word of God. You make it normal by reading and understanding that it is a prevailing theme throughout Scripture and it is a major recorded aspect of Jesus' ministry on Earth. So while it is very much supernatural, it is a humble submitted expectation to allow God to be God.

Jesus healed people and performed Miracles throughout the time of His ministry on this earth. This is consistent with God's character. There are Healings and Miracles in the Old Testament, as well. Therefore, ask and ye shall receive. Don't worry yourself with conflicting scenarios just yet. When you tell a kid that Moses' staff caused the Nile to turn to blood they don't try to explain it away. When you tell a kid that a woman just touched Jesus' clothes and was healed, they don't suddenly become a skeptic. Then why is it harder for adults to accept the supernatural work of our triune God? I think we have learned to protect ourselves from disappointment and it often becomes doubt and disbelief that He *will*.

So much of my upbringing in our little United Methodist Church was filled with praying in Faith for Healing for all kinds of people with all kinds of illnesses and afflictions. We prayed for Miracles too and we saw them! In fact, during a vacation bible school 20 years ago I sat in a metal folding chair and received a miracle as my pastor and my fellow confirmation students prayed for me. As a kid my left leg was shorter than my right by at least an inch. With legs stretched out straight in front of me and the hands of my friends laid on me we *watched*, actually saw beyond a shadow of a doubt, my left leg grow out to meet the right one. That day has been marked in our minds forever.

Training kids in Gifts of Revelation—Words of Knowledge, Words of Wisdom, and Discerning Between the Spirits—is similar to that of the Gift of Faith. It is providing them with a safe place to practice. There has to be an opportunity for them to step out in these Gifts and be encouraged and corrected. The New Testament has so many examples where these Gifts were in operation both in the ministry of Jesus and the disciples after He ascended. My parents always provided me with the freedom to speak my mind and that extended to spiritual things, as well. I had opportunity and a safe place to practice Words of Wisdom. It can be a discussion that is open for kids to share their thoughts. What you, or even they, think are their own thoughts could in fact be a Word of Knowledge or Wisdom or Discernment of a Spirit.

If these Gifts, just like the others, are discouraged and discounted as thoughts coming from themselves rather than revelation from the Holy Spirit, they will always be second guessing the Holy Spirit. Perhaps they will always keep it to themselves and never step out to be used by God for His glory in the Church. Most importantly, I believe, is teaching them to weigh what they and you may believe is one of these Gifts in operation with the Word of God. The influence of our own minds may interfere with a pure operation of these Gifts and so it is critical that they be judged by Scripture.

1 Corinthians 12 tells us about these Spiritual Gifts, that they are given to members of Christ's Church, are to be used in the Church, and that each individual serves a unique role in God's ministry through the Church to a dying world. The Gift of Knowledge is to be used to reveal God's own plan and purposes for an individual. This gift may highlight some fact of someone's life past or present as a way of revealing God's intimate concern for that individual. A Word of Knowledge is often a fact about someone that the giver of the Word could not possibly know. That gift in operation opens the door to minister to a person the love and care of Jesus. When a child receives a Word of Knowledge, it can seem a bit disconcerting. You should take that word before the Lord and weigh it in prayer with Scripture. Remember, it is your role to encourage and provide opportunity for practice. If you believe

that it is from the Holy Spirit, encourage the child to present that Word of Knowledge to an individual, if the word is specific enough, or to the congregation with the pastor's blessing. If it is not to be shared, it is a perfect opportunity to encourage the child to intercede in prayer for whoever needs that word.

The Gift of Words of Wisdom should be treated with the same reverence. Its purpose is to provide some of God's own wisdom to a situation that needs revelation. It could be the Church congregation as a whole that is facing a specific decision or an individual that needs to receive wisdom from on high to apply to their circumstance. This is easily weighed against Scripture because it is God's own wisdom, which we know He revealed through the Bible. Again, this Gift serves as an opportunity for ministry to people as it addresses a specific situation in which they find themselves. Teach the child to examine what they believe is a Word of Wisdom with the Word of God. If they still believe that it is from the Holy Spirit, then encourage them to share it. Giving a Word of Wisdom to someone can lift a huge burden from them in decision-making and give them God's clarity. It serves both the Church of Jesus and the non-believer by making God's interest in their life a manifest reality.

It is the Gift of Discerning Between Spirits that allows for supernatural ministry to an individual who needs deliverance in order to receive freedom in Christ. This Gift also allows us to discern between four different kinds of spirits. When children begin to move in this gift, you can help them by using the Word of God to distinguish between the different kinds of spirits they are discerning. This kind of insight into the spiritual world is absolutely for ministry purposes. Part of that ministry may be teaching a child to intercede in prayer for someone. If they begin to discern an evil spirit during a time of ministry for someone specific, they need to be encouraged to give that discernment to someone they can trust who will take it before the Lord to be weighed and measured.

The Gifts of the Holy Spirit that are made manifest through speaking out, such as Tongues, Interpretation of Tongues, and Prophecy, may require the most shepherding from parents for children. Like all of the other gifts, these require a safe place for practice, encouragement and opportunity to step out in the church community, and weighing it against the Word of God. I believe that understanding and explaining the purpose of these particular gifts to children is critical in equipping them to receive and move freely in them. These vocal gifts are the submission of the tongue of the person speaking to the utterances of the Holy Spirit. In other words, no matter which of these three Gifts are manifesting, they are being spoken through a person as God's own mouthpiece to be heard audibly. Hopefully you are already teaching your children how to hold their tongue when need be, to think before they speak, and in general use their words with kindness and purpose. They need to be taught how to discipline their tongue.

Hopefully, this is a Gift you can actually practice with your child. As you receive the Baptism of the Holy Spirit, Tongues will follow. I believe training your children in this Gift is very much like Healing. When you pray together, pray in Tongues. We must practice yielding our tongue to the utterances of the Holy Spirit within us. It is not natural to give up control in that way. Also, from my own experience, the more that I pray in Tongues, the easier it is for me to submit my tongue to the Holy Spirit's words and more syllables, various and different sounds begin to flow. This is great, because when I pray in English I am limited by my mind and by my native language to give words and meaning to my prayers. When I pray in Tongues, the Spirit within me is accessing intentions and meanings articulating them in prayer, unknown to my own mind, which perfectly address the heart and Will of God for a situation. Praying in Tongues gives your child access to a prayer life that is no longer limited by their mastery of their native language, their understanding of adult things, or their emotional or mental maturity. They are praying with supernatural insight into a spiritual world. This is powerful and teaching children to not be apprehensive about praying in Tongues will make them powerful prayer warriors.

The Interpretation of Tongues and the Gift of Prophecy fulfill the same purpose in the Church. An Interpretation of a Tongue serves the purpose of giving understanding and meaning to the unknown Tongue that has been spoken. Just like the Gifts of Revelation, these two Gifts require being weighed and measured, judged, against the Word of God. Children need to know how to do this themselves and you must train them to do that by taking them to Scripture when they come to you with these things. These Gifts are to edify, exhort, and counsel God's Church. Children must understand the importance of discerning whether what they are hearing and speaking is coming from God. Adults must impress upon kids the importance of discerning and then teach them how to judge it with Scripture.

I believe the more parents, teachers, and children/youth ministry leaders understand these Gifts themselves, the better equipped they will be to teach and train kids in the Baptism of the Holy Spirit and the Spiritual Gifts that accompany it.

About the Author

*"On your walls, O Jerusalem, I have appointed and
stationed watchmen (prophets), Who will never keep
silent day or night..."*
Isaiah 62:6 AMP

Rachel's life was a miracle—born the first and only child to two loving parents. It is clear that God ordained her to be an only child. Rachel was raised in church from a young age after her parents met the living God in a small United Methodist Church. At the age of 8, Rachel received the Baptism of the Holy Spirit while attending a good old fashioned Methodist revival service. By the age of 18, she was actively moving in Gifts of Faith, Healing, Miracles, and Discerning Between Spirits.

Rachel attended university and graduate school in Boston, MA where she studied Philosophy and focused on the discipline of Ethics. While a graduate student Rachel was reminded of her prophetic purpose while attending a prayer meeting at the Justice House of Prayer in Boston. This renewed her vision and passion to share her gift of teaching (Romans 12:7) with the Church.

Rachel has since returned home to Maryland where she currently serves as the Youth Ministries Coordinator at that same United Methodist Church from her childhood. Since 2011 Rachel has actively been serving to teach from Scripture in a variety of settings. She has always been deeply passionate about reaching into the pews, beyond religion, to ignite Christians with the fire of the Holy Spirit.

She seeks to find opportunities of ministry everywhere she goes. The Lord has graciously positioned her in places just to speak life into one individual. Since then, she has begun to move more frequently in Words of Wisdom, Words of Knowledge, and Prophecy.

The Lord has been ever kind and loving in confirming her prophetic purpose through the response of individuals who receive understanding and revelation under her teaching.

If you would like Rachel to speak at your Church, please contact her at lamplightingmin@gmail.com.

Feel free to connect with Rachel on social media:
Twitter—@lamplightingmin
Facebook—www.facebook.com/lamplightingmin

Made in the USA
Middletown, DE
25 May 2018